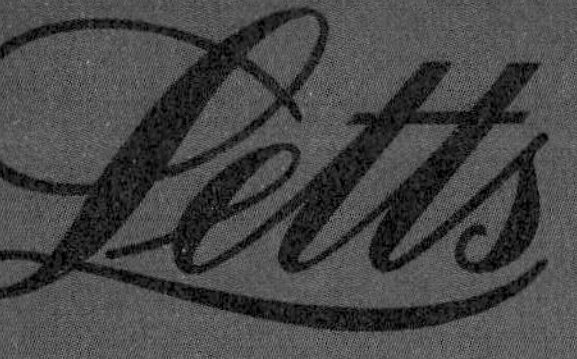

AS

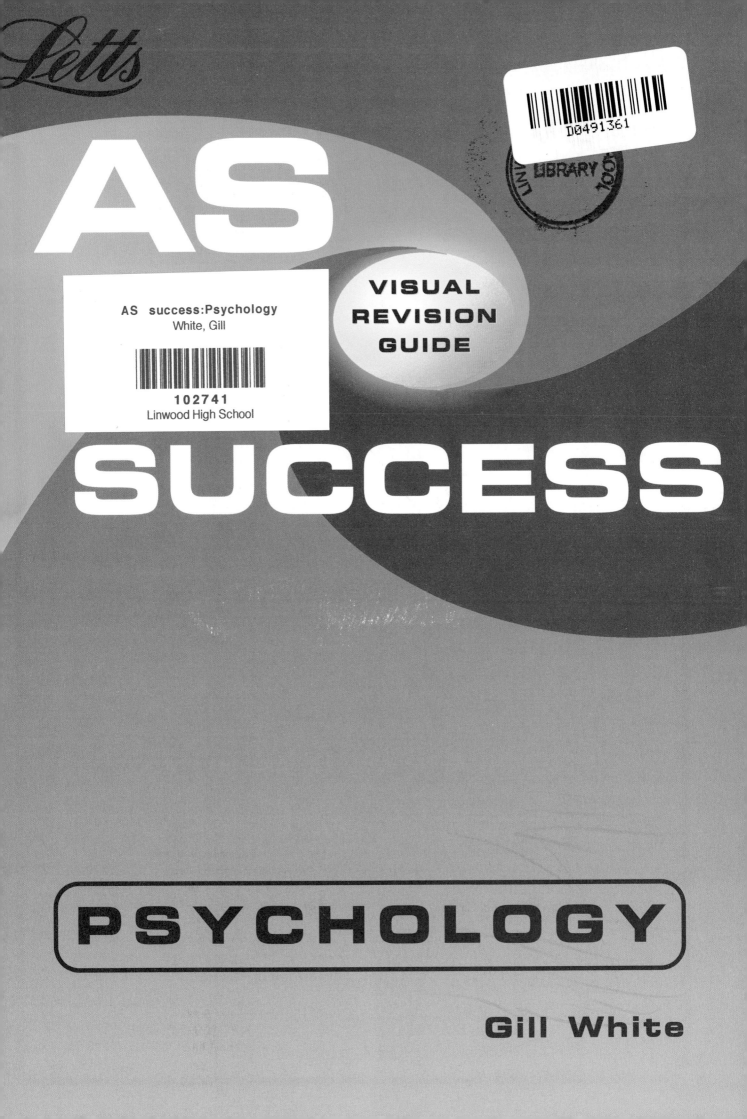

VISUAL
REVISION
GUIDE

SUCCESS

PSYCHOLOGY

Gill White

Contents

Social psychology

Physiological psychology

Individual differences

* OCR Core Study
** AQA – A Critical Issue

Introduction to AS psychology

The word psychology comes from the Greek '**psycho**', meaning 'mind', and '**logos**' meaning 'study of'. Psychology today involves the study of human behaviour, experience and mental processes. However, psychologists argue over precisely what should be studied and how it should be studied.

Psychologists approach the subject from many different perspectives and attempt to explain behaviour from many different angles.

Approaches to psychology

Freud

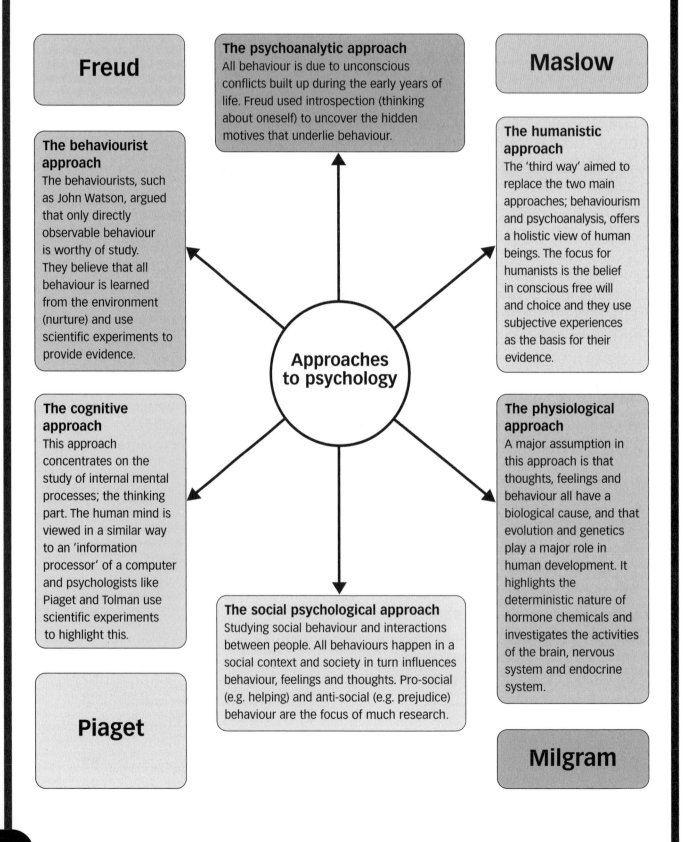

The psychoanalytic approach
All behaviour is due to unconscious conflicts built up during the early years of life. Freud used introspection (thinking about oneself) to uncover the hidden motives that underlie behaviour.

Maslow

The humanistic approach
The 'third way' aimed to replace the two main approaches; behaviourism and psychoanalysis, offers a holistic view of human beings. The focus for humanists is the belief in conscious free will and choice and they use subjective experiences as the basis for their evidence.

The behaviourist approach
The behaviourists, such as John Watson, argued that only directly observable behaviour is worthy of study. They believe that all behaviour is learned from the environment (nurture) and use scientific experiments to provide evidence.

The cognitive approach
This approach concentrates on the study of internal mental processes; the thinking part. The human mind is viewed in a similar way to an 'information processor' of a computer and psychologists like Piaget and Tolman use scientific experiments to highlight this.

Piaget

The social psychological approach
Studying social behaviour and interactions between people. All behaviours happen in a social context and society in turn influences behaviour, feelings and thoughts. Pro-social (e.g. helping) and anti-social (e.g. prejudice) behaviour are the focus of much research.

The physiological approach
A major assumption in this approach is that thoughts, feelings and behaviour all have a biological cause, and that evolution and genetics play a major role in human development. It highlights the deterministic nature of hormone chemicals and investigates the activities of the brain, nervous system and endocrine system.

Milgram

Nature versus nurture

An ongoing debate in psychology is the extent to which our behaviour, experiences and thought processes are due to nature or to nurture. Nature includes those aspects of humans that are innate (present at birth) and passed on through genes, therefore predetermined. Nurture refers to environmental factors such as social interactions, e.g. family upbringing and the wider society,

Determinism versus free will

Another issue is the extent to which our behaviour is determined for us. This can be due to nature (genetic predisposition) or to nurture (past experience), or even due to the situation in which the individual finds himself or herself. Free will, the extent to which we are free to choose, is difficult to measure or to prove.

Themes and issues within psychology

Methodology

The debate concerning how humans should be studied is filled with bias from all angles: gender, culture, society and historic context as well as the ethos of individual researchers and public opinion. The goal of identifying and isolating individual variables is constantly being sought by science, whilst humanists argue that this goal takes away the very essence of being human. The ethical nature of the methods used is also a controversial area of debate: does anything go in the name of science?

AS Psychology

The study of psychology at AS level involves a broad overview of many of the major areas as well as a critical look at the methods used to study them.

You need to know:

- Which approach is being taken.
- What is the main issue being highlighted.
- What conclusion was reached in each study and what does this tell us about human nature.
- What evidence is available to support each theory.
- What evidence is available against each theory.
- What is involved in each of the methods used.
- Which method was employed by each of the studies covered at AS.
- The advantages and disadvantages of each method.
- Alternative methods that could investigate the same research question but eliminate the major weaknesses of the original.
- How have the findings been applied to everyday life.

Know your exam board

Each board covers most of the areas within psychology, but they do so to varying degrees. This book covers material from all the boards, which can only help to broaden your knowledge further and aid in your understanding. Find out full details of the topics covered in your specification by speaking to your class teacher and visiting the appropriate exam board online at:
www.ocr.org.uk
www.aqa.org.uk

Exam technique

Remember that psychology examiners are looking for evidence of your knowledge and understanding. There is rarely one 'right' answer to a question.

OCR focuses on 20 Core Studies, highlighted in the Contents by *. Exam questions focus on both detail of studies and the wider issues they raise.
Cognitive psychology: memory; perception; language; autism.
Developmental psychology: conservation; personality; institutionalisation; aggression.
Social psychology: obedience; social roles; discrimination; helping behaviour.
Physiological psychology: localisation of brain function; brain lateralisation; dreaming; emotions.
Individual differences: racial identification and preference; intelligence; schizophrenia; Multiple Personality Disorder.
Methodology: covered throughout as each Core Study is evaluated.
A practical investigations folder to complete.

AQA – Specification A focuses on three modules with a Critical Issue raised in each sub-section. These are highlighted in the Contents by **. The exam will include essays from each section, including the Critical Issues.
Module 1: Cognitive psychology (memory) = Eyewitness testimony.
Developmental psychology (attachment) = Day care.
Module 2: Physiological psychology (stress) = Stress management.
Individual differences (abnormality) = Eating disorder.
Module 3: Social psychology (social influence) = Ethical issues is psychological research
Research methods: Quantitative and qualitative research methods; research design and implementation; data analysis.

AQA – Specification B focuses on three modules that are slightly different from Specification A. See your teacher and the website.

Methodology: Experiments

The aim of psychology is to study human behaviour and experience. There are many ways of doing this. Each method has its own advantages and limitations and the most appropriate choice will depend greatly upon what the psychologist is investigating. Often a combination is used in order to provide a wider picture and stronger evidence.

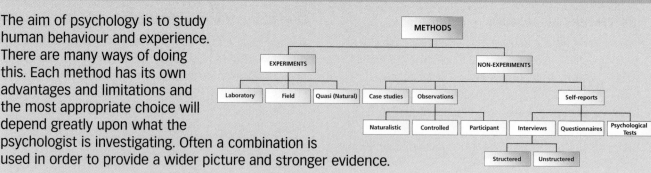

- METHODS
  - EXPERIMENTS
    - Laboratory
    - Field
    - Quasi (Natural)
  - NON-EXPERIMENTS
    - Case studies
    - Observations
      - Naturalistic
      - Controlled
      - Participant
    - Self-reports
      - Interviews
        - Structered
        - Unstructered
      - Questionnaires
      - Psychological Tests

Experiments

- Experiments are used to test theories and to look for differences between conditions.
- Variables are anything that varies – either naturally or through manipulation.
- One variable is manipulated (the **independent variable**) into two or more conditions.
- The effect this has on another variable (the **dependent variable**) can then be measured.
- If **extraneous variables** do escape the controls put in place they can confound the results; they are then referred to as **confounding variables**.

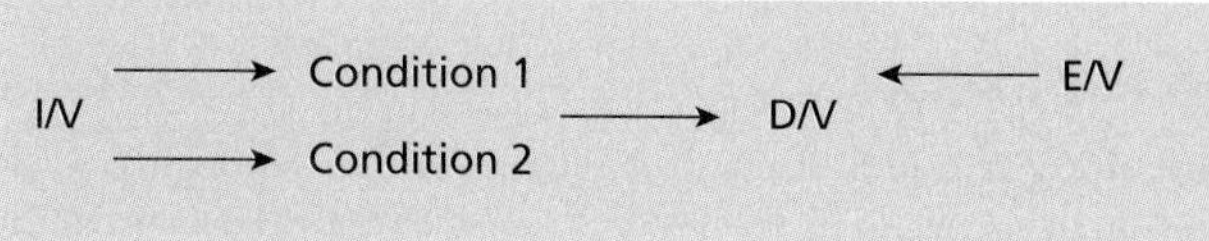

Controls

Laboratory experiments

An independent variable is **deliberately** manipulated and its effects upon the dependent variable are measured. Strictly standardised instructions are used as control for extraneous variables.

Advantages:

- Good control over extraneous variables means **cause and effect** can be identified.
- Controlled conditions also increase **objectivity**, i.e. not open to personal interpretation.
- Standardisation increases **replicability** (can be repeated).
- Replicability means results can be verified.

Limitations:

- The artificial location may **cause** participants to behave unnaturally.
- Participants may respond more to the demands of the situation, i.e. to its **demand characteristics**. This can include trying to please the experimenter or deliberately trying to behave in the opposite way to what is expected.
- The results may not generalise to real life, i.e. lack **ecological validity**.

Example (Bandura et al. 1961):

Does watching violence **cause** children to be aggressive?

- Two variables = observed violence and aggression.
- The independent variable = violence (determined **independently**, i.e. before the experiment begins).
- I/V can be split into conditions – e.g. violent and non-violent, so some children watch violent model and some watch non-violent model.
- The effect this has on the levels of aggression shown (dependent variable) can then be measured. Results **depend** upon the condition the children were in.
- Extraneous variables, such as different levels of aggression before the experiment, must be controlled, or the results will be confounded. Children with equal levels of aggression could be selected.

Field experiments

The independent variable is deliberately manipulated in a more natural setting under natural conditions. Participants can be unaware that they are taking part in an experiment.

Advantages:

- Greater ecological validity as participants are in their own natural environment.
- Less demand characteristics if unaware of taking part.

Limitations:

- Less control over extraneous variables, which can **bias** the results.
- Difficult to replicate exactly.

Example (Bickman 1974):

Does the perceived authority of a person giving orders affect the likelihood of obedience?

- Pedestrians asked by male experimenters to comply with requests such as 'pick up the bag for me'.
- The independent variable was the way the experimenter was dressed.
- The dependent variable was the number of people complying with the request.

Quasi (natural) experiments

The independent variable (e.g. gender, age, race) is naturally occurring (therefore not manipulated by the experimenter).

Advantages:

- Greater ecological validity because the independent variable occurs naturally.
- Less demand characteristics if unaware of being tested.

Limitations:

- No control over the independent variable or over extraneous variables means cause and effect are harder to identify.
- Impossible to replicate.

Example (Hraba & Grant 1970):

Does a person's race influence their self-identity and racial preference?

- Independent variable = race (black = light, medium and dark; white = others).
- Independent variable = time (results were compared to Clark's original study).
- The race of the interviewer was controlled.
- Dependent variables = racial preference, racial identification and racial self-identification.

EXAMINER'S TOP TIP

Experiments can collect data in various ways. Read the question carefully so you write about the right thing.

Quick test

1. ***Why do researchers use experiments?***
2. ***What is an 'independent variable'?***
3. ***What is the term given to describe the extent to which the results of a study can be generalised to real life?***
4. ***What are demand characteristics?***
5. ***Why might an experimenter choose to carry out a field experiment?***
6. ***What is the major weakness of a quasi/natural experiment?***

1. To identify differences between conditions and thereby to identify causal relationships (cause and effect). 2. The variable that the researcher manipulates. 3. Ecological validity. 4. Participant responds to the demands of the experimental situation (positively or negatively) rather than behaving naturally. 5. In order to increase ecological validity and decrease the possibility of demand characteristics. 6. Lack of control over variables.

Methodology: Non-experiments

Non-experimental methods include case studies, observations, self-reports, and correlations.

EXAMINER'S TOP TIP
Learn to evaluate different methods – it's a very useful skill.

Case studies

In-depth study, usually long term, of an individual or a specific group. Often used to investigate unusual or rare behaviour such as natural cases of human deprivation or rare psychological disorders (e.g. **Multiple Personality Disorder**). Research often involves interviews and observations or occasionally psychological tests.

Advantages:

- In-depth and detailed data is collected.
- Researcher gets to know the participant well.
- Can be short-term or long-term (longitudinal).
- High **ecological validity**.
- Findings can identify areas for further research.

Limitations:

- No cause and effect can be identified.
- Often relies on memory of the individual and so can be **unreliable**.
- Can be difficult to generalise to the rest of the population as a single case study is **biased** and uses an **unrepresentative** sample.
- Impossible to replicate.
- Relies on interpretation of findings by the researcher (researcher bias).

Example:

Curtiss 1989 investigated the effects of privation by using a case study of Genie, a young girl who had spent most of her childhood locked in a bedroom in her home. Without contact with the outside world she did not develop physically, cognitively or socially.

Observations

These can be **naturalistic**, **controlled**, or with the researcher as a **participant**.

Naturally occuring behaviour is observed in the participants' natural environment. Variables are not manipulated in naturalistic observations, but can be in controlled observations.

- Humans studying humans will give biased results as every researcher has their own perspective on the world (**observer bias**).
- Two or more observers reduce the chances of biased results so the findings are more reliable (**inter-observer reliability**).

Advantages:

- High ecological validity **if** the participant is unaware of being observed.
- No demand characteristics.
- Detailed and in-depth data.
- Replicable if controlled.

Limitations:

- No control over extraneous variables makes cause and effect difficult to identify.
- Ethical issues of deception and invasion of privacy.
- Observer bias.
- Researcher's presence can influence participant's behaviour if participating in observation.

Examples: Natural

- Lorenz's research into imprinting.
- Studies into children in day-care.

Controlled

- Sleep patterns.
- Ainsworth's strange situation.

Participant

- Rosenhan's 'Sane in insane places'.

Self-reports

These include interviews, questionnaires, and psychological tests.

- They rely on the individual's conscious thoughts and therefore will not access unconscious motives and defence mechanisms – see Freud.
- They can rely on memories of events, thoughts and feelings and therefore are prone to unreliable answers – see Bartlett and Loftus and Palmer for 'reconstructive memories'.

Questionnaire
Question 1...
What is the answer?
a) Something
b) Something else
c) Don't know
Question 2...
What is the next answer?
a) Either
b) Not sure
c) Yes
Question 3...

Interviews – Can be structured (pre-determined questions) or unstructured

Involve questioning participants verbally and recording responses.

Advantages:

- Can collect large amounts of data regarding internal mental states, relatively quickly.
- Flexibility, depends upon degree of structure.
- Often produces quantitative data that is easy to score and analyse.
- Replicability depends upon degree of structure.

Limitations:

- Results can be biased by socially desirable answers or by motivational levels.
- Cause and effect cannot be identified.
- Answers need interpretation.
- Too structured can ignore data, as answers are restricted.

Questionnaires

Written methods of recording participants' responses to set questions. Can be used for attitude or opinion surveys.

Advantages:

- Closed (yes/no) questions are easy to score and analyse.
- Replicable.
- Can collect huge amounts of data relatively quickly.

Limitations:

- Bias due to **acquiescence** (agreeing with items).
- Bias due to **response set** (always replying in the same way).

Psychological tests

Personality or intelligence tests.

Advantages:

- Standardised for a population, which ensures reliability.
- Replicable.

Limitations:

- Difficult to devise reliable tests.
- Difficult to devise valid tests – construct validity.

Quick test

1. *For what areas or human experience or behaviour are case studies most often used?*
2. *As a 'participant' observer, what would be your greatest difficulty?*
3. *How could an observer ensure reliability?*
4. *Which non-experimental method identifies causal relationships?*
5. *What is 'response set'?*
6. *Why are self-reports unreliable?*

1. Rare or unusual behaviour. 2. Researcher's presence can influence participants' behaviour. 3. By comparing results to another observer – 'inter-observer' reliability. 4. All methods are open to interpretation, so identifying cause and effect is difficult; findings are usually subjective. 5. Replying in the same way throughout a questionnaire. 6. No access to unconscious thoughts and feelings, unreliable memories, unmotivated individuals, demand characteristics and social desirability.

Research design

Generation of appropriate aims

- **A clear theory will specify variables and the association between them.**
- **Research aims are specific questions the researcher plans to answer.**

Formulating different types of hypothesis

Experimental hypothesis

- A **hypothesis** is a precise, testable statement – a prediction of what the researcher expects to find.
- A more specific hypothesis may be easier to test – but may be difficult to generalise to other situations.
- A more general hypothesis may be easier to apply to many situations – but may be more difficult to measure.

Example:
'Children taught the new reading scheme will attain a higher score on the end of year reading test than children who use the old reading scheme'.

EXAMINER'S TOP TIP
Use these terms as often as possible when evaluating methodology.

- **Directional or one-tailed**: the hypothesis predicts the direction of the effect. E.g. It predicts that performance will 'improve'.
- **Non-directional or two-tailed**: the hypothesis predicts a difference but not its direction. E.g. 'Children taught the new reading scheme will attain a *different* score on the end of year reading test than children who use the old reading scheme'.

Null hypothesis

- Predicts that study results will be due to chance alone, not to the effects of the independent variable.
- Inferential tests are used to decide the statistical probability of the results being due to chance.

Reliability

The reliability of a test refers to how dependable and consistent it is in measuring.

- **Internal reliability:** how consistently a method measures within itself. Can use the **split-half method**:
  - Random split
  - First ½ and second ½
  - Odds and evens

  } If high correlation found then reliable.
- **External reliability**: how consistently a method measures over time. Can use the **test-retest method** – if high correlation found then reliable.

Validity

This is the extent to which the experiment measures what it is supposed to.

- **Face/content validity**: examining the content of the test. Does it look correct in the eyes of an independent researcher? This can be subjective.
- **Concurrent validity**: collect results from new method and compare to old method.
- **Construct validity**: validating a hypothetical construct, e.g. intelligence. Can the new method be used to support the underlying theoretical constructs?
- **Predictive validity**: test should predict future results.
- **Ecological validity**: does the test measure behaviour that could occur naturally?

EXAMINER'S TOP TIP
Ask yourself, 'Is there anything else I could have been measuring'? E.g. people's concentration levels.

Variables

A variable is anything that may change. Scientific research requires that variables should be clearly defined.

Operational variables

- Exact and precise descriptions of the variables in question.
- Operationalising narrows the focus of the research: e.g. 'Will improve memory' is not measurable; 'Will remember more words' is.

Weaknesses in the methodology

- Unwanted (**extraneous**) variables may influence the results and must be controlled for. They can be the result of
  - **random error**: unpredictable; results from the participants' state of mind, levels of motivation, or from environmental conditions such as temperature and noise.
  - **constant error**: more predictable and may effect one condition more than another, so it must be controlled for. It may result from differences between the participants that have not been taken into account or order effects.

Minimising effects of situational variables

Situational (extraneous) variables are those aspects of the research setting that might influence the performance of participants, such as aspects of the task, the physical environment, or personal factors.

Replicability

The extent to which procedures can be replicated.

- **Standardisation** helps to ensure that measurements are accurate.
- Standardising the procedures – e.g. instructions and procedures given to participants need to be identical.
- Establishing a set of standards (norms) for a test.

Order effects

Responses may be due to the order in which the conditions were carried out. They may be positive effects, through practice or learning, or negative effects, that arise through boredom.

- **Counterbalancing** is a possible solution to the problem of order effects. Equal numbers of participants undertake the tasks in different orders.
- **Randomisation** is an alternative solution. The order of presentation of experimental conditions is decided by a random strategy such as drawing lots or tossing a coin.

Demand characteristics

These are responses influenced by the demands of the situation, e.g. participants may try to respond how they think the experimenter wants them to or set out to deliberately confound the results.

Individual difference effects

Responses may be due to individual differences between people.

Generalising

This is the extent to which the results from the sample can be generalised to other people. Depends upon sample bias, validity, reliability, experimenter effects, etc.

Quick test

1. ***What is a hypothesis?***
2. ***What is wrong with the hypothesis 'watching violent TV makes children aggressive'?***
3. ***Write an operationalised hypothesis for the above statement.***
4. ***What is 'internal reliability' and how would you check for it?***
5. ***What are 'order effects' and how can you reduce them?***

1. A precise and testable statement that predicts what the researcher expects to find. 2. The variables are not operationalised (measurable). What sort of violent TV? What is meant by 'aggressive'? 3. 'Children who watch Power Rangers will hit other children at school more than children who do not watch it'. 4. How consistently a test measures – use 'split-half' test to find a correlation. 5. Responses may be due to the order the conditions were carried out (practice or boredom). Reduce through counterbalancing or randomisation.

Samples and design

There are two key concepts in the selection of participants:

- **Population: a group of people who share a given set of characteristics, e.g. all students on an A level course.**
- **Sample: the population is usually too large, so a representative sample must be used.**

Random sample

Each person in a given population stands an equal chance of being selected.

Advantage: Selection is unbiased and best chance of gaining a representative sample.

Limitation: Sample may not be random – just selected in an unbiased way.

Stratified sample

Arranged in layers: (a) proportions of the important factors in the total population are ascertained (e.g. age, social class); (b) sample size and participants represent the distribution of these factors in the target population.

Advantage: Attempt to identify most important factors to research.

Limitation: Time-consuming.

Self-selected sample

Participants select themselves, e.g. by replying to adverts (Milgram 1960).

Advantage: Convenient and ethical.

Limitation: Selectivity of response – sample will be atypical and biased.

Opportunity sample

Researcher selects anyone available at the time, e.g. at college or at work.

Advantage: Very widely used – simple and convenient.

Limitation: Extremely biased and unrepresentative.

Experimental designs

Independent measures

Different participants are used in each condition, e.g. one group of children receive a new reading scheme and other group do not.

Advantages

- No order effects as each participant only does one condition.
- Demand characteristics unlikely.

Limitations

- Individual differences between participants.
- More participants are needed.

Repeated measures

Same participants are used in each condition.

Advantages

- Individual differences are eliminated.
- Fewer participants are needed.

Limitations

- Order effects will require counterbalancing.
- Demand characteristics are an issue.

Matched pairs design

Different participants are used in each condition but they are **matched** as closely as possible, e.g. matched on age, reading ability, etc.

Advantages

- Individual differences are reduced.
- Order effects and demand characteristics are reduced

Limitations

- Individual differences can never be completely eliminated.
- Time-consuming and requires more participants.

Non-experimental designs

Observations

These require behaviour to be categorised. Categories should be decided before observation begins to ensure consistently recorded data.

- **Observational grids** are devised containing behavioural categories to be ticked.
- **Rating systems** – each participant is rated in terms of the degree of behaviour shown, e.g. degree of frustration.
- **Coding systems** – symbols or abbreviations are used to record categories of behaviour quickly.

Sampling techniques

- Event sampling: a frequency count is kept of the number of times an event or specific behaviour occurs.
- Time sampling: observations made at certain time intervals, e.g. once every minute.
- Point sampling: individual's behaviour recorded only until enough data has been collected.

Questionnaires

- Consider the minimum information required to ensure completion.
- Ensure questions are answerable.
- Open-ended questions collect in-depth information – qualitative.
- Fixed choice – easy to quantify and code but limits participants' answers.

Likert scales are common for collecting data on attitudes as they measure the strength of an attitude.
Example: How far do you agree with this statement:
A level exams are too difficult?

Strongly agree	Agree	Don't know	Disagree	Strongly disagree
1	2	3	4	5

Interviews

- Need to be planned; can use structured pre-set questions or open-ended questions.
- How information will be recorded – tape recordings allow later re-analysis for reliability.

Researchers – participant relationship

- **Investigator effects**: investigator's expectations may influence participant's behaviour and interpretation of results.
- **Hawthorne effect**: if an individual is aware of being observed, they may improve performance.
- **Greenspoon effect**: individuals may be influenced by the investigator's comments.
- **Demand characteristics**: responses may be influenced by the demands of the situation.
- **Evaluation apprehension**: participants are anxious about being tested, try to guess what is required and behave accordingly.

Ways of reducing these effects

- **Single-blind technique**: does not inform participants of the true aim of the experiment.
- **Double-blind technique**: does not inform either participant or experimenter of the true aim.
- **Placebo technique**: gives a control group a treatment that should have no effect.

EXAMINER'S TOP TIP

Bias caused by the people involved in a study is always a good evaluation point to raise.

Quick test

1. *What is meant by a 'representative' sample?*
2. *Which design reduces order effects and individual differences?*
3. *What is 'time sampling'?*
4. *What is a 'Likert scale'?*
5. *What is the 'Hawthorne effect'?*
6. *Why would a 'double-blind' experiment improve the validity of a study?*

1. A sample that truly represents the target population – not biased in favour of any individual or group. 2. Matched pairs 3. Observations made at certain time intervals, e.g. once every minute. 4. Scales that measure the strength of an attitude. 5. A change in an individual's behaviour due to being observed. 6. Bias is reduced on both sides and it's more likely to measure naturally occurring behaviour.

Ethical issues

In the past psychologists have been expected to judge for themselves whether or not their investigation is going to upset, hurt or damage their participants. Now, both the British Psychological Society (BPS) and the American Psychological Association (APA) have issued guidelines for all researchers (from top psychologists to students carrying out practicals).

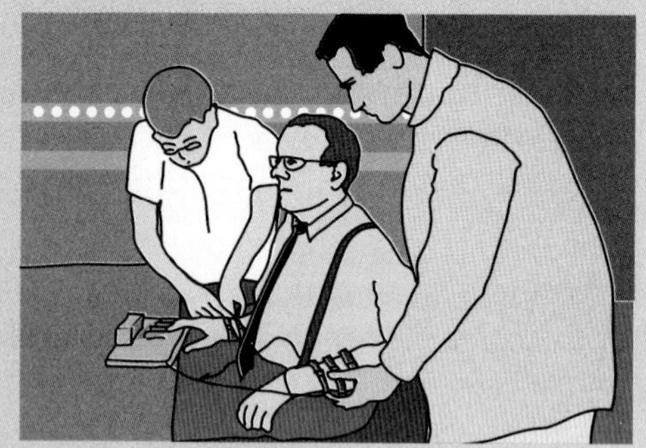

Milgram deceived participants into electrocuting others!

Ethical issues in human research

Informed consent

All participants should be fully informed about all aspects of the study before they begin in order to consent to taking part. This inevitably alters the behaviour of participants and can bias the results due to demand characteristics.

Deception

Participants should not be deceived unless there is no other way of studying the topic in question. Should not be used for trivial research. In order to overcome ethical objections to deception the following two methods can be used:

- **Prior general consent**: a pool of volunteers consent to being deceived in some future experiment.
- **Presumptive consent**: approval from the general public can be gained prior to an experiment.

Debriefing

After the study, participants should be fully informed of all aspects of the research, e.g. what the study tells us about them, what the results will be used for, etc. This is vital if deception has been used. Participants should leave the study in the same state as when they arrived.

The right to withdraw

It is important that participants are fully aware of their right to withdraw from the study at any point. This is true right up to the very end of the research, even if all data has been collected.

Protection of participants

All participants should be protected from physical harm and psychological harm. This includes long-term effects such as embarrassment or stress as well as short-term.

Confidentiality

All personal information about the participants should be kept confidential; use pseudonyms or simply number each person, e.g. Eve Black and Eve White (Multiple Personality Disorder).

Colleagues

All psychologists (and students) are responsible for each other. If you consider a study to be unethical, it is your duty to report this to the BPS (or APA).

Sensitive research

Be aware of how the results of your study may be used by others. For example, intelligence tests given to army recruits in the First World War highlighted the 'fact' that different races have different intelligence levels. This led to strict immigration laws being put into place and added fuel to the eugenics argument. It was later discovered that the tests were in fact culturally biased, but by then the damage had been done (see Gould).

Weigh up the **costs** (to the participant) and the **rewards** (knowledge gained)

'The ends justify the means' – Stanley Milgram, 1963

Ethical issues in animal research

Law

In the UK it is illegal to cause pain or distress to any animal. The only exception to this is if the experimenter gains a 'Home Office Licence' that allows certain procedures to be carried out.

Costs and rewards

Weigh up the costs of suffering to the animal with the rewards (knowledge gained). The decision to allow any suffering is one that can only be made by the Home Office (see 'Law').

Caging conditions

The conditions in which the animal is kept must take into account the social behaviour of the species. The smallest number of animals possible should be used.

Species

Some species will suffer under certain conditions whilst others will not. Be sure to know as much as you can about the particular species investigated and consider if another species would give the same results without such harm being caused.

Endangered species

Any species that is 'endangered' should not be considered for psychological research (either under laboratory conditions or in the wild).

EXAMINER'S TOP TIP

Lack of informed consent and deception are not appropriate guidelines for evaluating studies on animals.

What you need to know

Evaluate the core studies covered in AS psychology on ethical guidelines (i.e. which guidelines did the experimenter follow and which were broken).

Task: Look through the studies and consider the research procedures from an ethical viewpoint.

Quick test

1. ***Under what conditions would the use of deception be acceptable?***
2. ***What is the purpose of debriefing?***
3. ***Why is gaining informed consent not always possible?***
4. ***How did Milgram justify the deception he used to persuade his participants to 'electrocute' fellow participants?***
5. ***What must a psychologist obtain if he wishes to carry out research on an animal that may potentially cause distress to the animal?***
6. ***Is the fact that an animal cannot give informed consent to take part in a study justification for not using animals?***

1. When there is no alternative. 2. To return the participants to the same psychological state in which they entered the study.
3. If participants are aware of the purpose of the study they may respond to demand characteristics and behave unnaturally.
4. The ends justify the means. 5. A licence from the Home Office. 6. No! Might seem common sense but it is not part of the ethical guidelines.

Data analysis 1

Qualitative data

- Data in descriptive form.

Observations

- Definitions of behaviour need to be operationalised.
- Important to record all behaviour of interest.
- If possible, context in which behaviour occurred should be recorded.

Questionnaires

- Open-ended questions can produce in-depth descriptions of subjective matter.
- Analysis will be subjective.

Interviews

Data can include:

- What actually happened – context and behaviour observed.
- Participant interpretations – self reports of behaviour or cognitions.
- Researcher interpretations of above.

Case studies

Data can include

- All behaviour and interpretations of behaviour should be recorded.
- Often focus in on one or two specific issues.

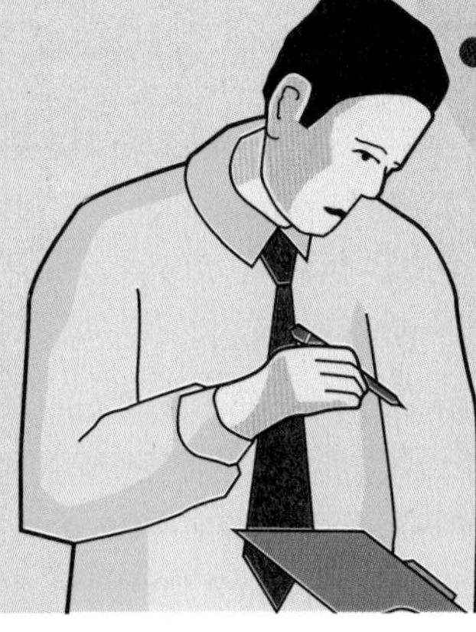

Remember: data from non-experimental methods can also be quantified.

Quantitative data

- Data in numerical form.
- **Nominal data**: data measured roughly by counting the frequencies of occurrences in specific categories, e.g. male/female or helping/not helping.
- **Ordinal data**: only indicates the order of results, e.g. 1st, 2nd, 3rd. The interval between each rank position is unknown.
- **Interval**: data on a scale – has an accurate value. The intervals between each value are equal, e.g. temperature.
- **Ratio**: interval data with a true zero, e.g. time or length.

Levels of significance

Inferential tests can be applied to numerical data to discover the probability that the results are due to chance. A significance level of 5% ($p \leq 0.05$) is usually accepted by psychologists. This means that the probability of the results being due to chance is 5% and the probability of them being due to the variable in question is therefore 95%.

Measures of quantitative data

Measures of central tendency and dispersion

Quantitative data can be summarised through descriptive statistics. There are three main measures of central tendency; they provide an average figure that summarises the data.

Mean

Average = add up all scores and divide by number of items, e.g. 1,3,5,5,6,6,6,7,7,8 = 54/10 = 5.4. Use with interval data.

- **Advantage:** most useful measure as it takes into account all data values.
- **Limitation:** decimal places may be meaningless (e.g. 2.2 children!).

Median

Middle value of scores when arranged in order, e.g. 1,3,5,5,6,6,6,7,7,8 = 6. Use with interval or ordinal data.

- **Advantage:** use the median when unsure about reliability of extreme values, as it remains relatively unaffected.
- **Limitation:** not suitable for use with small data sets.

Mode

Most often occurring value, e.g. 1,3,5,5,6,6,6,7,7,8 = 6. Use with nominal data (or ordinal/interval).

- **Advantage:** the mode does appear in the data values.
- **Limitations:** slight changes in a small number of scores can completely change the mode; it does not tell us anything about the other values in the data set.

Measures of dispersion describe the spread of the data

Range

Difference between the lowest score and the highest score (add 1 if all scores are whole numbers; add 0.1 if scores are to one decimal place; add 0.01 if to two decimal places, etc.).

- **Advantage:** quick to calculate and takes into account extreme values.
- **Limitation:** does not take into account individual values and provides no information on the distribution of scores around the mean or median.

Standard deviation

Measures the spread of data around the mean. To calculate the square root of variance:

1. Calculate the mean, e.g. sum of scores (Σx) divided by number of participants.
2. Subtract the mean from each individual score.
3. Square each of the resulting scores.
4. Add up all the squared scores.
5. Divide the total by 1 less than number of participants = variance.
6. Square root of the variance = standard deviation (SD).

- **Advantages:** takes into account all values in a data set. Inferences can be made about probability based on the difference between the standard deviation and a normal distribution curve.

Two thirds of a normally distributed population (68.26%) fall within one SD of the mean, 95.44% fall within two SD and 99.73% fall within three SD.

- Each single figure summarises quantitative data and therefore can ignore individual scores.
- Measures of central tendency and dispersion can be subjected to inferential statistics and therefore inferences can be made about probability.

Quick test

1. *Data collected via interview needs to distinguish between what?*
2. *If comparing how many people study psychology with how many people study philosophy, what type of data would be collected?*
3. *What measure of central tendency would best describe the results of the above study?*
4. *When would the mean be the most appropriate measure of central tendency to use?*
5. *What is a 'measure of dispersion'?*
6. *Measures of IQ are normally distributed. What percentage of the population falls within 1 SD of the average?*

1. What actually happened, participants' subjective interpretation and researchers' interpretation. 2. Quantitative and nominal.
3. Mode, e.g. **most** people study psychology compared to philosophy. 4. When the data is interval.
5. Describing how spread out the data is. 6. 68.26%.

Data analysis 2

Graphical representations and statistics

Visual displays summarising measures of central tendency are useful ways of describing data. Easy to read – providing of course that everything is clearly labelled and titled. Axes should be labelled carefully as their manipulation can produce very different visual displays.

Bar charts

If scores are in the form of categories (nominal), data can be represented visually through bar charts.

- Only those categories that are of interest to the researcher are indicated.
- Categories are indicated along the horizontal axis and frequencies indicated along the vertical axis.
- Categories can be arranged in either descending order (most popular to least popular) or ascending order (least to most).
- Categories can be arranged in alphabetical order (which is less biased).
- The frequency scale can begin at zero or higher, depending upon the usefulness of the scale (if lower scores are missing, this must be indicated).
- The frequency columns usually represent number of times a category was recorded but can also represent the mean scores or percentages of different groups.

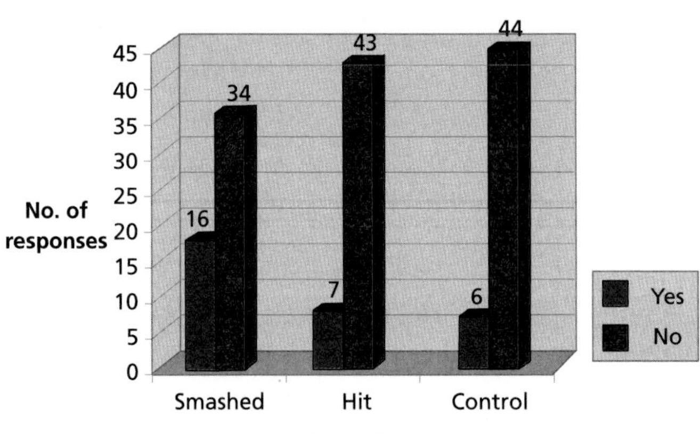

Histograms and polygons

If scores can be ordered (ordinal, interval or ratio), data can be represented visually through histograms and polygons.

Histograms

- Scores in ascending order are always placed along the horizontal axis.
- Frequencies of the scores (number of individuals obtaining this score) are placed along the vertical axis.
- Column blocks show the frequencies.
- All scores are shown even if no frequency was recorded.

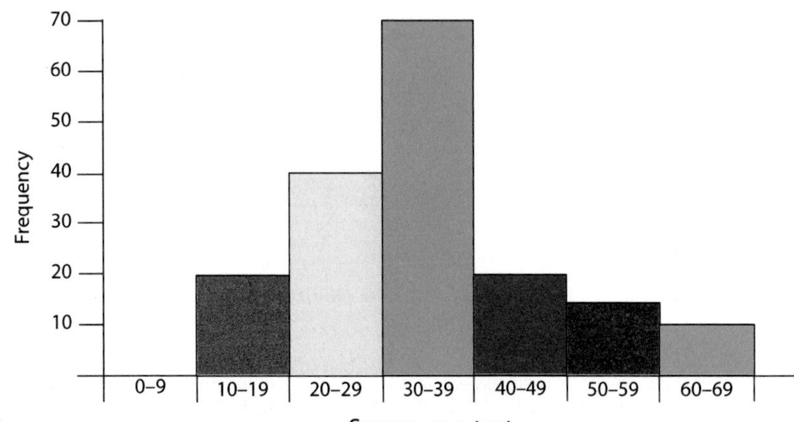

Shows data for all categories, even those with zero values. The column width for each category interval is equal so the area of the column is proportional to the number of cases it contains of the sample.

Frequency polygons

- These are similar to histograms with scores placed along the horizontal axis and their frequency along the vertical axis.
- As for histograms, it is important that the intervals are not too narrow or too broad.
- As opposed to histograms, individual points indicate scores. Useful when two different frequency distributions need to be compared.

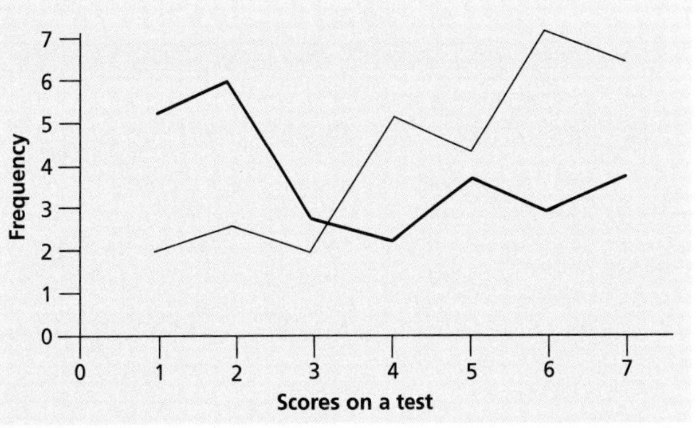

Correlations

A way of analysing data already collected. Two sets of data (co-variables) are collected from an individual and the degree of relationship between them is ascertained.

Advantages:

- No manipulation of behaviour is needed.
- The **strength** of a relationship between two or more variables can be measured.
- Strong relationships can often highlight areas for experimental research that will then determine cause and effect.

Limitations:

- No cause and effect can be identified (a relationship does not indicate what is causing what).

Scattergraphs

- Correlations can be represented visually using a scattergraph (scattergram).
- One set of scores is indicated on the horizontal axis and the other on the vertical axis.
- Each individual's scores is indicated by a single point:
  a positive correlation shows that as one variable rises, so does the other;
  a negative correlation shows that as one variable rises the other falls.

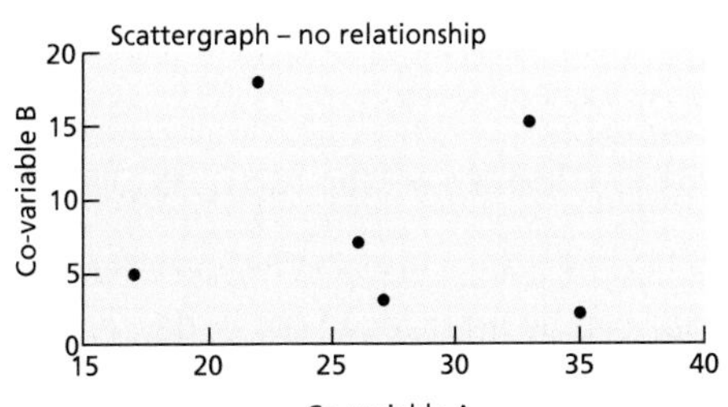

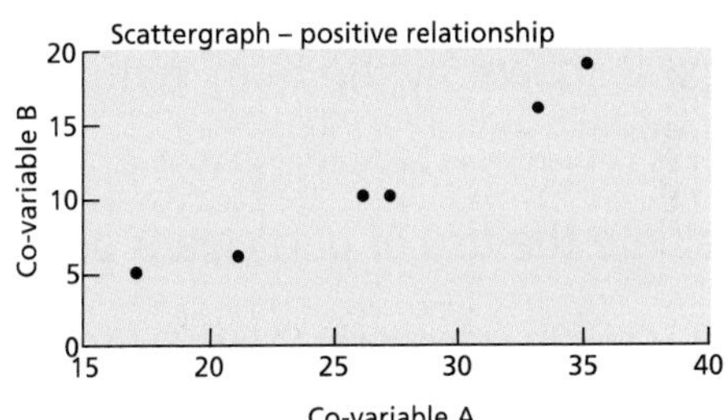

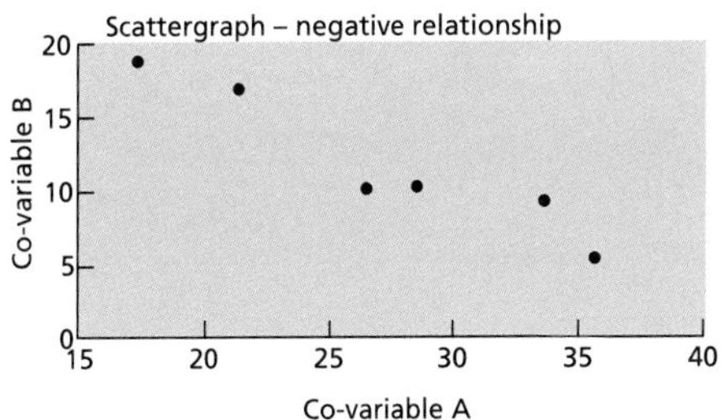

- A correlation coefficient is calculated to give a more precise measure of the relationship between the two variables and the degree of probability.

Quick test

1. ***When would you use a bar chart to represent your data?***
2. ***What advantage does a polygon have over a histogram?***
3. ***What is usually presented on the vertical axis of a graph?***
4. ***When would you use a scattergraph?***
5. ***What would a correlation coefficient measure?***
6. ***If a negative correlation was found between college attendance rates and final results at AS level, could we infer that low attendance causes low results?***

1. When the data is nominal (categories). 2. Polygons can be used to compare two different frequency distributions. 3. Frequency of occurrence. 4. To display a correlation visually. 5. The degree of probability that the results are significant (i.e. not due to chance). 6. No. We cannot infer any cause and effect from correlations. There may be a third variable involved but not yet discovered.

Practice questions

Use these to test your progress. Check your answers on pages 92–95.

Research methods in psychology

1 What are experiments used for? [2]

....

2 What is meant by the term 'independent variable'? [2]

....

3 What is meant by the term 'extraneous variables'? [2]

....

4 Why is it important to standardise the instructions in a laboratory experiment? [2]

....

5 What is meant by the term 'ecological validity'? [2]

....

6 What is the difference between a field experiment and a natural experiment? [2]

....

7 What is meant by the term 'naturalistic observation'? [2]

....

8 Evaluate the use of participant observations. [4]

....

....

....

9 How can a researcher reduce observer bias? [2]

....

10 What are the major limitations of self-reports? [4]

....

....

....

11 What is meant by the term 'one-tailed' hypothesis? [2]

....

12 What is meant by the term 'null hypothesis'? [2]

....

13 How can a researcher decide the probability of the results being due to chance? [2]

....

14 What is meant by the term 'construct validity'? [2]

....

....

15 How can a researcher check the reliability of the results? [2]

....

16 Give an example of a constant error, and state how it might be reduced. [2]

....

17 How can a researcher select a representative sample from a given population? [2]

....

18 What is meant by the term 'independent measures' design? Evaluate its use. [4]

....

....

....

....

19 What is the placebo technique? [2]

....

20 What are the seven major ethical guidelines in human psychology? [3]

....

....

....

21 What ethical guidelines are given for research using animals? [3]

....

....

....

22 What is meant by the term 'qualitative data'? What are its limitations? [3]

....

....

....

23 When is it appropriate to represent data using a histogram or polygon? [2]

....

24 What is the major limitation of a correlation? [2]

....

25 What is meant by the term 'correlation coefficient'? [2]

....

Total /59

Memory: Short term and long term

Psychologists study the cognitive processes of memory, e.g. how memories are stored. Evidence from studies of brain-damaged individuals supports a distinction between short-term and long-term memory, as well as different kinds of short-term memory.

Short-term memory

Encoding

Short-term memory uses a mainly **acoustic code** – sound, e.g. by repeating the material verbally. **Conrad 1964**: rhyming letters are harder to recall than non-rhyming letters because of acoustic confusion errors. This research may lack ecological validity; a possible problem for all memory research.

> List (a) is easier to recall than list (b):
>
> (a) G S Z W N T R
>
> (b) D E C G P B T

Capacity

Miller, 1956 used span measures and discovered that short-term memory has a limited capacity of about seven items: **'the magical number seven, plus or minus two'**. Chunking can increase this capacity: seven items are still remembered but each 'item' is larger – easier if the units have meaning. Capacity for short-term memory can also be seen in **recency effects**, showing higher recall for the last few items in a list.

> List (a) is harder to recall than list (b):
>
> (a) R A C R A F F B I B B C (12 items)
>
> (b) RAC RAF FBI BBC (4 items)

Duration

The **Brown–Peterson** technique is a means of demonstrating duration of short-term memory.

Trigram experiment

- Ask participants to remember a single nonsense syllable of three consonants (e.g. JTP).
- Give them an interference task to prevent rehearsal.
- Test recall after various times (e.g. 3,6,9,12,15,18 seconds).
- Good recall after 3 seconds (80%) decreasing to around 10% after 18 seconds.

Long-term memory

Encoding

Baddeley 1966 suggests that long-term memory uses **semantic coding** (meaning of words).

> After 20 minutes list (a) is harder to recall than list (b) as words with similar meanings are confused:
>
> (a) small, little, tiny, minute
>
> (b) pit, test, event, card

Capacity

Unlimited (impossible to measure).

Duration

Tested using very long-term memories (VLTMs) studies.

- **Ebbinghaus** tested memory of nonsense syllables after delays of 20 minutes to 31 days. Found that a large proportion of information was lost very quickly and then stabilised to a slower rate of loss.
- **Linton** recorded events from her life each day over 6 years and then randomly tested her own recall of them. She found a much more even and gradual loss of data over time (approx. 6% per year).

Varieties of long-term memory

Distinctions are important for criticising the validity of memory research.

- **Procedural knowledge** is 'knowing how' – implicit memory, e.g. how to talk, walk, ride a bike. Often cannot describe them to other people.
- **Declarative knowledge** is about 'knowing that' – explicit memory. Easier to describe and therefore more useful in memory research. It can be:
  - **Episodic memory** – this is concerned with events and people.
  - **Semantic memory** – this contains knowledge about language, meaning and general facts.

Models of memory

These offer accounts of information transfer from short-term to long-term memory.

The multi-store model of memory: Atkinson and Shriffrin 1968

- The first information-processing model distinguishing between separate sensory, short-term and long-term memory stores.
- Transfer through verbal rehearsal.
- Influential model – supported by research.
- Too simplistic and inflexible and not true of real-life memory performance.

Stimuli perceived → Sensory memory → (coding) → Short-term memory (Rehearsal) → (coding) → Long-term memory

Sensory memory ↓ Information lost if not attended to

Short-term memory ↓ Information lost e.g. via decay

Long-term memory ↓ Information lost e.g. via interference

The working memory model: Baddelely and Hitch 1974

- Focuses on representing short-term memory and active processing (compare with multi-store model).
- STM operates more like a working memory – a flexible and complex system of components (shown below).

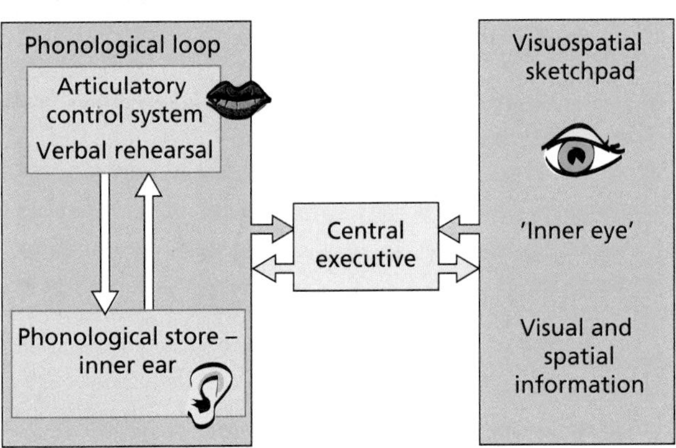

- Influential model supported in many experimental studies (e.g. if two tasks are being performed at once and one interferes with the other, they must use the same component).
- Criticised for lack of evidence about the precise role and functioning of the central executive.

Levels of processing model: Craik and Lockhart 1972

- The crucial factor in forming memories is the amount and depth of processing they receive.
- Material processed more deeply will be remembered better.
- Has received empirical support in experimental conditions.
- Problems with defining 'deep' processing.
- It describes but does not explain memory processes.

'Depth' can be provided through (MODE)

Meaning = understanding the meaning of information, rather than rehearsal.
Organisation = putting information into categories.
Distinctiveness = unusual words are recalled better than common 'everyday' words.
Elaboration = complex semantic processing recalled more than simple processing.

EXAMINER'S TOP TIP

Be prepared to explain what is meant by the terms used on page 22, to outline a model of memory or to explain differences between models.

Quick test

1. *How is information encoded in short-term and long-term memory?*
2. *How can you improve your short-term memory?*
3. *Why did Peterson's trigram experiment require the use of an interference task?*
4. *According to Craik and Lockhart's theory, what should you do with information in order to recall it more easily later?*
5. *How can you produce deep processing?*
6. *What evidence is there for the various components in Baddeley and Hitch's 'working memory model'?*

1. Short term = acoustic; long-term = semantic. 2. Chunking: can still only remember 7 units but make each unit bigger by putting similar items together. 3. To prevent rehearsal, which may allow information to transfer into long-term memory. 4. Pay attention to it and consider it deeply. 5. MODE = **M**eaning, **O**rganisation, **D**istinctiveness, **E**laboration. 6. When performing two tasks at once, if one interferes with the other they must use the same component.

Memory: Forgetting

Forgetting may be due to a lack of availability (the material is not there to be retrieved) or a lack of accessibility (material cannot be accessed – e.g. tip of the tongue). Forgetting in STM seems to be due to decay or displacement, whereas forgetting in LTM seems to be due to retrieval failure or interference.

Forgetting in short-term memory (STM)

As STM has limited capacity, forgetting is likely to be due to lack of availability.

Decay theory

- Memories have a physical basis known as a trace.
- This trace will decay in time unless it is passed on to the LTM.

Diversion of attention is similar because it assumes that time is the factor in forgetting; if attention is drawn to something else the original trace will decay.

Displacement

- A limited capacity store can lose information because it has been replaced by newer material.

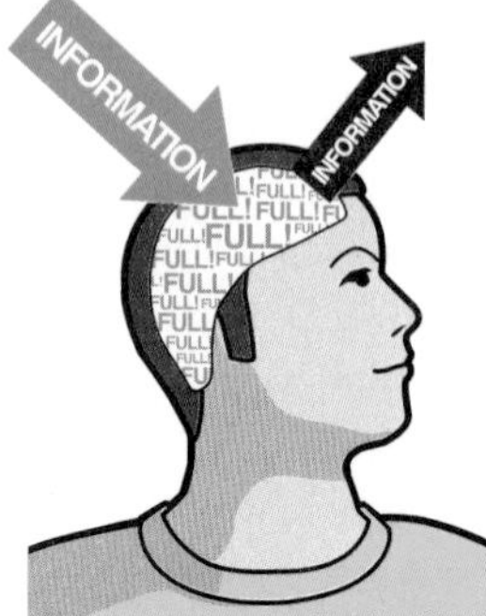

Interference

- Interference tasks (e.g. as used by Peterson) will displace the original material to be learned.

Forgetting in long-term memory (LTM)

- Trace decay may also occur in LTM through disuse; knowledge or skills can fade if not used.
- Motor skills, such as riding a bike, never seem to fade. Involve a continuous skill where each action acts as a cue for the next – Baddeley 1999.
- More complex motor skills such as resuscitation, however, that also require accurate knowledge, have been shown to decline if not practised (McKenna and Glendon 1985).
- Seems unlikely that decay through time is the only factor in forgetting.

Interference

- Forgetting increases the more similar the interference material is to the original.
- **Retroactive interference**: new information interferes with old information.
- **Proactive interference**: an old memory trace disrupts new information – Underwood, 1975.
- All experiments are laboratory-based and therefore lack ecological validity.

Accessibility

- Memory is available (it has been stored) but it can not be accessed. Can be due to **retrieval failure**:
- Tip of the tongue phenomena – Brown: people tend to remember the first letter of target word and the correct number of syllables.
- Cue-dependent forgetting (Tulving and Psotka 1971) can occur if the correct retrieval cues are not available. If subjects are given cues (e.g. categories), there is better access to memory.

The role of context

External context: Abernethy 1940

- Cues in the environment act as cues for jogging the memory.
- Students tested in the same room in which they were taught, with their usual lecturer, did better than students tested in a different room with a different lecturer.

Internal context

- Internal cues such as mood state can act as cues to jog memory.
- Recall improved when there is a match between the mood at the time of learning and the mood at the time of retrieval.

Emotional factors

Cognitive theories can be accused of ignoring emotional factors in memory processes, but it is probable that how we feel will influence accessibility of memories. Highly emotional states can lead to **'flashbulb' memories** whilst painful memories may be repressed into the unconscious mind.

Flashbulb memories – Brown and Kulik 1977

- Some memories for important events appear to be remembered with great clarity. These flashbulb memories may be more accurate and longer lasting because of hormones produced at times of high emotion. This might suggest that such memories have an adaptive function.
- However, some psychologists such as Neisser reject the idea that flashbulb memories are special in any way and believe that they are subject to the same kinds of distortion and forgetting as other memories for events.

Repression – Freud 1915

- **Repression** is a defence mechanism that occurs as a result of increased anxiety.
- Anxiety-producing memories (e.g. traumas such as sexual abuse) are repressed into the unconscious mind, which may explain forgetting.
- Hypnosis may uncover repressed memories.

Amnesia

A loss of memory, usually as a result of brain damage, which may occur through ageing, illness (or alcohol consumption), injury or surgery.

Retrograde amnesia

- A form of amnesia resulting from brain injury in which the individual loses memories for the time period just prior to the injury. It is loss from LTM, as in the case of Clive Wearing who lost information prior to the onset of herpes.
- The time period may be from a few minutes to several years, and typically it is worst for events that occurred just before the injury.

Anterograde amnesia

- Unable to transfer new factual information between STM and LTM.
- Caused by brain damage to the hippocampus.

Case study of HM after removal of hippocampus (in order to control his epileptic seizures): was then unable to form new long-term memories.

Evaluation of studies involving brain damaged patients must consider the lack of **generalisability**. These 'patients' are atypical and whilst helping to isolate component parts of memory, they may not be applicable to 'normal' people.

EXAMINER'S TOP TIP
Make sure you can define important terms.

Quick test

1 ***What are the two main reasons for forgetting in STM?***
2 ***What is meant by the term 'displacement'?***
3 ***What are the two main reasons for forgetting in LTM?***
4 ***Why do skills such as resuscitation fade after time, whilst skills such as bike riding do not?***
5 ***What two types of contextual cues can affect memory?***
6 ***What are flashbulb memories?***

1. Decay and displacement. 2. STM can be lost because it has been replaced by newer material. 3. Retrieval failure and interference. 4. Resuscitation skills decline if not practised as they are more complex and require accurate knowledge as well as motor skills (McKenna and Glendon 1985). 5. External cues in the environment (e.g. recall in same room as learnt) and internal cues such as recalling information when in same mood state as when learnt. 6. Very clear and accurate memories produced because of hormones produced at times of high emotion.

Memory: Eye witness testimony

Eye witness testimony (EWT) has been shown to be unreliable. Explanations for inaccuracy seem to revolve around the reconstructive nature of memory (schema theory) and the influence of language on memory (leading questions).

Reconstructive memory (Bartlett 1932)

- **Schema theory** suggests that general knowledge influences what you remember and learn.
- A schema (block of knowledge) contains generalised knowledge built up from **past experience**.
- Schemas affect **recall** because they affect both initial learning (comprehension) and subsequent **retrieval**.
- Memory retrieval involves an active process of reconstructing, which is then **biased** by information already contained in the schema.
- Cannot account for occasions when memory is extremely accurate.

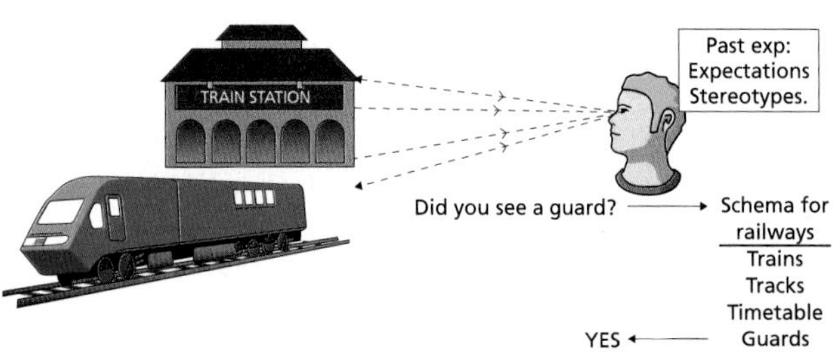

Evidence for Bartlett's theory

- Asked people to learn a piece of text containing information that conflicted with their expectations.
- Recall after 20 hours showed considerable changes in both content and style of the story (e.g. English participants replaced 'canoe' with 'boat').
- The transformations continued over time, indicating that memory was continually being reconstructed.
- Research criticised for lack of experimental control but the concept of schemas continues to be important.

Face recognition

This is an important but **often unreliable** element of eyewitness testimony.

- Whilst **recognising familiar faces** is a fairly simple task for most people (participants recognised classmates from 35 years earlier) **[Bahrick et al 1975]**), recognition of an unfamiliar face, seen perhaps only once, is much more difficult.
- **Distinctive faces** are easier to recall.
- Reading a face **holistically** is also easier than recalling it feature by feature – Identikit pictures may not be effective because they are based more on feature detection than arrangement and they are unmoving.

Emotional state

Emotions of witnesses at the time of a crime may also lead to unreliable memories.

- **Flashbulb memories** may account for improved recall of some events due to **high emotion** at the time. **E.g. Johnson and Scott 1978**: laboratory experiment with low stress and high stress conditions – high stress (carrying letter-opener covered in blood) led some participants to be better at identifying the offender.
- Alternatively, extreme **negative emotion** may create repressed memories. E.g. hypermnesia refers to enhanced memory allegedly bought about by hypnosis; **Putnam 1979** found participants questioned under **hypnosis** made **more errors** than those who were not – suggestible hypnotic state may allow memory to be influenced by leading questions.
- Controversy surrounding recovery of **repressed memories**: some psychologists believe that 'false memories', which are then believed to be true, may be placed into the participant's mind – **ethical implications**.

Applications

- Research into EWT has helped police to improve the collection and use of eyewitness testimony.
- The **Cognitive Interview** increases contextual cues and reduces eyewitness anxiety.
- Psychologists can be used as expert witnesses in criminal trials to advise jurors on the reliability of eyewitness testimony.

Reconstruction of automobile destruction – Loftus and Palmer 1974

Aim

To investigate the effects of leading questions on the accuracy of speed estimates and accuracy of memory of a car crash.

Method

Two laboratory experiments.

Experiment 1

Participants: 45 students were shown a film clip of a car accident.

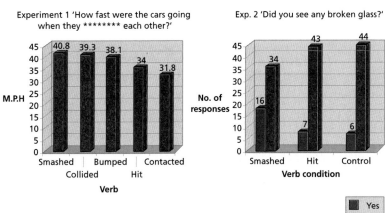

Critical question: "How fast were the cars going when they ******* each other?"

Independent variable (I/V): the verb used in the question;

5 conditions – smashed, collided, bumped, hit, contacted.

Dependent variable (D/V): the estimated speed.

Experiment 2

Participants: 150 students tested 1 week after film clip.

I/V: 3 conditions – smashed/hit/control.

Critical question: "Did you see any broken glass?"

D/V: whether or not broken glass was seen (NB no broken glass appeared in the film).

Strengths

- Control over extraneous variables such as view of scene, distractions, enables cause and effect to be identified.
- Standardised procedure means study is replicable.

Weaknesses

- Biased sample: students used therefore lacks generalisability.
- Relies on self-reports.
- Lack of ecological validity – artificial environment and film not of a real accident.
- Possibly induces demand characteristics.

Alternative

- More random sample to improve generalisability.
- Field experiment: real-life car accident, maybe at a race track – improves ecological validity, however less control over extraneous variables such as emotional factors.

Results

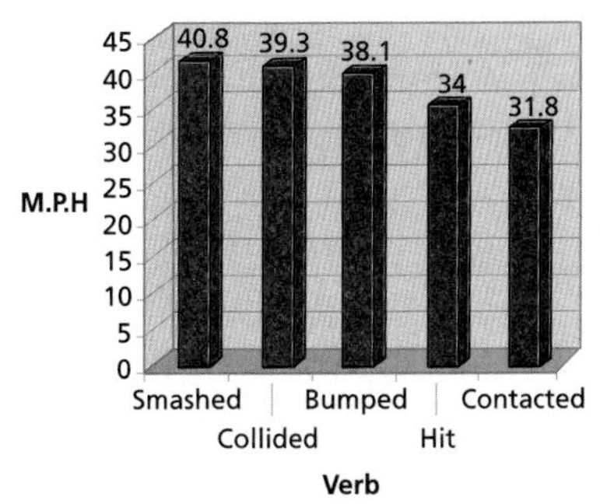

Exp. 2 'Did you see any broken glass?'

No. of responses

45 40 35 30 25 20 15 10 5 0

16 34 7 43 6 44

Smashed Hit Control

Verb condition

Yes

No

Conclusion

- The verb 'smashed' increases the estimates of speed, and the likelihood of seeing broken glass that was not present.
- Provides support for reconstructive memory.
- Memory itself is transformed at the time of retrieval.

Application

- Devlin Report (1976): judges required to instruct jury not to convict on a single eye-witness testimony (except relative/close friend).
- No leading questions in courtroom.
- Cognitive interviews – help people to recreate the whole context.

EXAMINER'S TOP TIP

When evaluating studies state the point and then explain what this means.

Quick test

1. *According to schema theory, what is the main influence on our memory?*
2. *Why did the English participants in Bartlett's study change 'canoe' to 'boat'?*
3. *Why did Johnson and Scott's participants have better recall of confederate holding the letter-opener?*
4. *Why is the sample in Loftus and Palmer's study biased?*
5. *Why did the verb 'smashed' lead to a higher estimate of speed?*

1. Past experience and general knowledge. 2. 'Boat' fits more with their schema. 3. This condition created high stress (blood and therefore a flashbulb memory. 4. Students are unusual; all similar age and they use their memories a lot more than other people. 5. The severity of the verb suggests a higher speed and this combines with original memory.

Perception and attention

Bottom-up perception

The world is 'out there' to be seen – Gibson. In 1960, Gibson and Walk's 'Visual cliff' experiment demonstrated an innate ability to perceive depth. However, the case study of SB, who had his sight restored after many years but was not able to perceive depth, suggests learning.

Top-down perception

The world is constructed and therefore influenced by past experiences (see Bartlett's schema theory of memory) – Gregory.

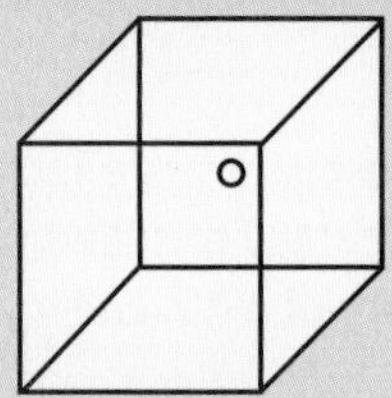

The 'switch' you see is evidence for Gregory.

Nature versus nurture

Cross-cultural studies enable us to discover the extent to which perceiving is structured by the nervous system (and so common to all human beings) – **nature** – and to what extent by experience – **nurture**.

William Hudson: 'the key to understanding pictures lies in depth cues'. We **learn** three rules:

- Rule one = larger objects are perceived as nearer.
- Rule two = overlap – obscured objects seen as further away.
- Rule three = perspective – lines converge as they get further away (e.g. railway lines).

Müller-Lyer illusion – Rivers 1901

- With arrow shafts pointing outwards the centre line is perceived as longer.
- Murray Islanders less prone to Müller-Lyer = carpentered world hypothesis = we live in a man-made environment full of straight lines therefore we are more prone to non-conscious use of depth cues.

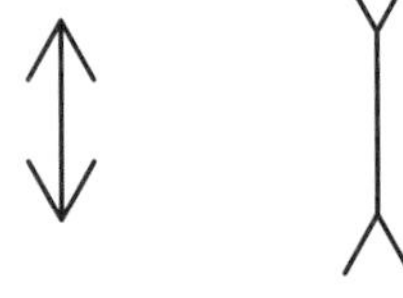

Is the left vertical really shorter?

The Müller-lyer illusion – the line on the right appears longer than the other as the arrow heads are used as depth cues.

Attention

Selective (focused) attention

The ability to focus on one particular stimuli or task while ignoring others.

Broadbent's filter model (1958): Single channel attended to at a time.

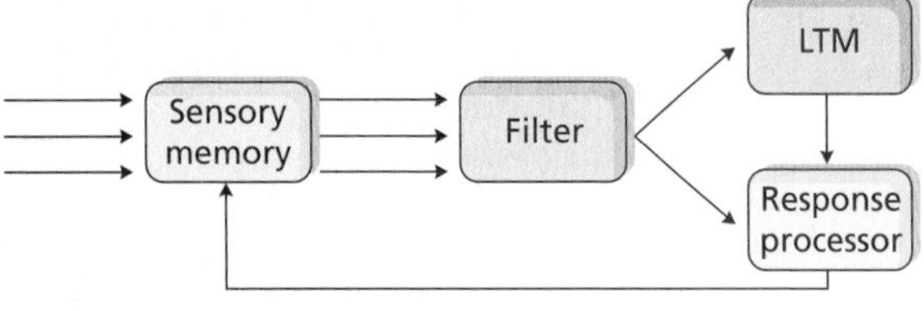

✔ Evidence from 'split span task'.
✘ 'Channel' not explained clearly; Gray and Wedderburn (1960) showed two channels processing together.

Triesman's attenuation model (1964): Attenuating filter – unselected channels weakened, not blocked out completely.

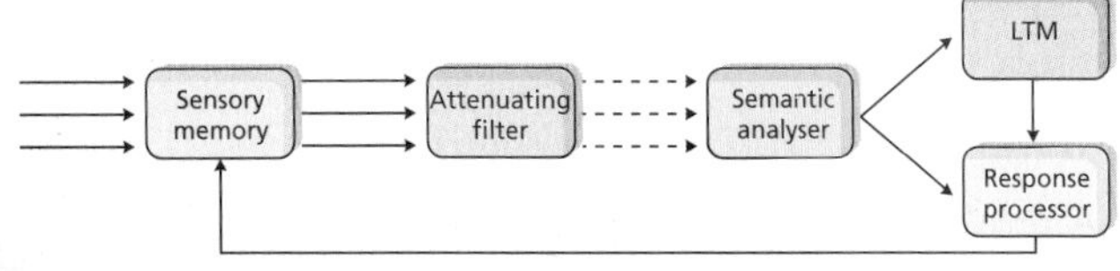

✔ Evidence: 'cocktail party' phenomenon.
✘ 'Attenuator' is not explained clearly.

Deutsch and Deutsch's pertinence model (1963): Late filter – after the meaning has been analysed.

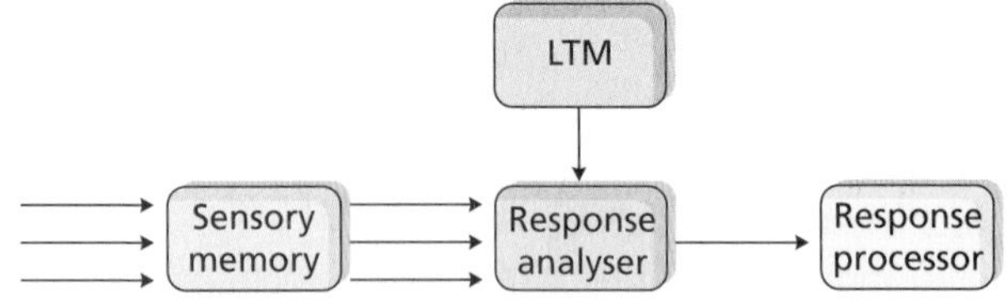

✔ Evidence: Gray and Wedderburn (1960) – all analysed semantically and in parallel.
✘ Earlier research suggests meaning of unattended stimuli is not processed.

Divided attention

Carrying out more than one task at a time.

Kahneman's general capacity model (1973)

- Central processor allocates attention to each task.
- If total demand exceeds capacity, some tasks will not be attended to.

✔ Explains how automatic tasks can be carried out simultaneously (Spelke 1976).
✘ Stroop effect' shows how automatic processes interfere with attention and therefore suggests we are not free to allocate attention.

Cross cultural perception – Deregowski 1972

Aim

To review studies showing that different cultures perceive pictures differently.

Method

Deregowski performed a review of a series of 'cross-cultural studies'.

Study 1: Laws & Frazer – late 19th-century missionaries.

- Showed a profile picture of a human head – African women didn't recognise it as it only had one eye.

Study 2: William Hudson's (1972) famous picture.

- Spearing the antelope or the elephant? Africans could not say which animal was 'being speared'.
- They did not seem to use depth cues and were classed as two-dimensional viewers.

Study 3: William Hudson 'making models'

- Shown picture of two squares connected by a 'rod' and asked to build a model.
- British schoolchildren try to build three-dimensional models (boxes).
- Two-dimensional viewers built 2-D models.

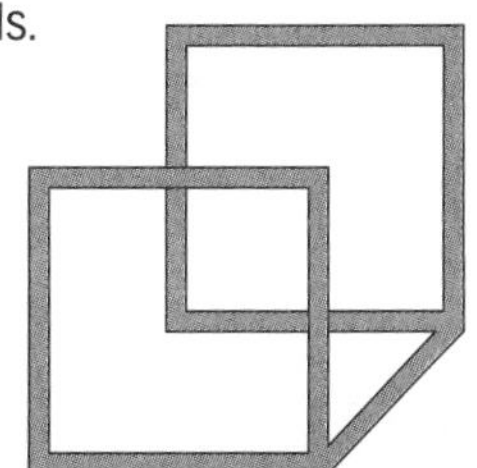

Study 4: The impossible trident

- 3-D viewers found it harder to draw – they spent longer looking at it (trying to make sense of it and build a 3-D image in mind).

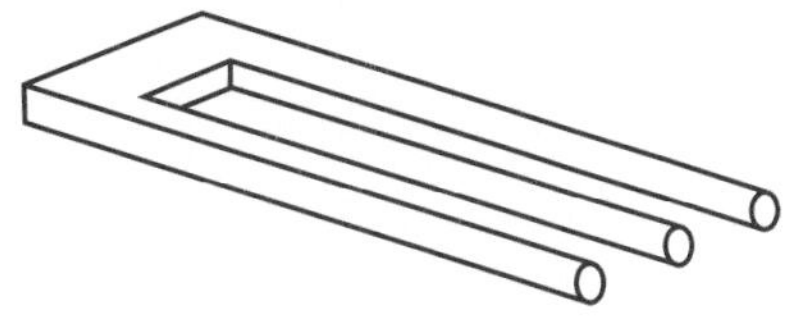

Study 5: Richard Gregory

- Unskilled African viewers adjust a spot of light so that it lies at the same depth as an object in the 'spearing the antelope' picture.
- Movement was only side to side and not forward, regardless of depth of object on picture.

Study 6: Split-style drawing

- African children preferred the split style.
- Westerners preferred the perspective drawing.

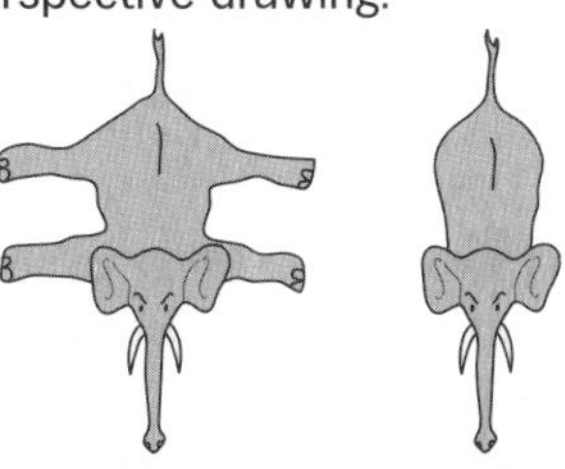

Strengths

Cross-cultural studies are not a method but an approach.

- Good attempt to study cultural differences.

Weaknesses

- Deregowski says Laws & Fraser (Study 1) was unsystematic.
- Natural (quasi) experiments – little control over extraneous variables such as individual differences.
- Ethnocentrism – regarding one's own group (culture) as the 'norm' for comparison.
- Imposed ethics – devising a method in one culture and using it on another (e.g. Africans unfamiliar with pictures drawn on paper).

Conclusions

Different cultures use different rules to construct their pictures and they perceive them differently – suggests that some form of learning is involved in this process.

Applications

- Better insight into human perceptual processes.
- Improvement in communication across cultures.

EXAMINER'S TOP TIP

Try to use the six studies to back up the conclusion reached.

Quick test

1. *What evidence is there that perception is learned?*
2. *What criticisms can be made of Broadbent's filter model of attention?*
3. *Why couldn't the Africans say which animal was being speared?*
4. *What is meant by the term 'ethnocentrism'?*
5. *Why do Westerners find drawing the trident impossible?*

1. Switch in Gregory's cube; also cross-cultural studies have found differences. 2. Gray and Wedderburn (1960) showed two channels processing together. 3. They did not seem to use depth cues. 4. Regarding one's own group (culture) as the 'norm', against which other groups should be compared. 5. They try to make sense of it and build a 3-D image in their mind.

Thinking

Thinking is the mental processing of concepts (internal representations). Individuals have different cognitive styles influencing the way they perceive, think about and store information.

Two main styles identified by Guilford in the 1950s:

- **Convergent thinking**: focus on a single best solution to a problem by bringing information together (deductive reasoning). Works better when problems have unique solutions.
- **Divergent thinking**: produces one or more novel ideas relevant to the problem. There is no 'correct' solution: therefore works better for open-ended problems.

Insight – Kohler (1925) used chimpanzees and discovered that divergent thinkers can sometimes solve problems with a sudden flash of insight.

Reasoning is a kind of logical problem-solving that involves drawing conclusions from the information to hand. It can be:

- **Inductive** – specific cases are used to generate a general rule.
- **Deductive** – general rules are used to make specific inferences.

Representation of knowledge

Knowledge of the external world must be made internal. It is represented in the mind through schemas or **schemata** – blocks of knowledge (of concepts, objects, events) that are able to store information about a specific object, behaviour, etc., which can change and assimilate new information and adapt to accommodate it.

Hierarchical model of concept organisation

Collins and Quillian (1969) suggest that knowledge is represented in a **hierarchical semantic network**.

Representations can be visual images or auditory 'scripts' of knowledge. Stored knowledge influences what new information is attended to and the thinking processes that follow.

Animal
Has skin
Breathes
Eats

Bird
Has feathers
Has wings
Can fly

Canary
Is yellow
Can sing

Fish
Has gills
Has fins
Can swim

Trout
Is brown
Can be eaten

EXAMINER'S TOP TIP

Studying things that have gone wrong is useful for telling us how 'normal' thinking develops.

Autism

Cognitive processing involving thinking can sometimes develop 'abnormally', into autism.

- Most severe of child psychiatric disorders (Kanner, USA, and Asperger, Austria, 1943).
- Affects 1–2 per 1 000 and 2–4 times as many boys as girls.
- Usually detected from age 4 years and seems to be life-long.

Autistic symptoms

Autism can be seen on a continuum:

Low functioning ⟷	High functioning
Many symptoms	Some symptoms
IQ < 70	Not mentally impaired

Sufferers often show 'islets of ability'.
Three important impairments:

- Social interaction.
- Communication.
- Repetitive and stereotyped patterns of behaviour, and lack of normal imagination.

Past theories of autism

- Bettelheim (1967) – Psychoanalytical Approach = poor parenting.
- Lovass (1979) – Behaviourist = concentrate on symptoms rather than cause.
- Tinbergen (1983) – Ethological = interactions within families; avoidance/approach motivations.

Does the autistic child have a 'theory of mind'?
– Baron - Cohen, Leslie and Frith 1985

Aim
To find whether autistic children lack 'Theory of Mind' – the ability to attribute beliefs to others.

Method
A **natural** or **quasi** experiment.

I/V: three groups of children; autistic (20 aged 11 years, mental age 5 years), Down syndrome (14 aged 10 years, mental age 5 years), and 'normal' (27 aged 3–5 years).

The Sally Anne Test:

- Experimenter shows children two dolls; one called Sally and one called Anne.
- Children asked if they could name dolls (Naming question).
- The dolls are then shown acting out; Sally puts a marble in her box and goes out for a walk (Sally is hidden).
- Anne plays a trick on her; she takes the marble from Sally's box and places it into her own box.
- Sally is brought back and children asked:
  - 'Where will Sally look for the marble?' (Belief question).
  - 'Where was the marble in the beginning?' (Memory question).
  - 'Where is the marble really?' (Reality question).

Results

Question	Percentage of correct responses		
	Autistic	Down	'Normal'
Naming/reality/ memory	100	100	100
Belief	20	86	85

- The belief question, 'Where will Sally look for her marble?', is the **critical** question: 80% of autistic children failed to respond correctly compared to only 14% of Down syndrome and 15% of 'normal' children.

Conclusion
- Autistic children do not have a **theory of mind** (ToM).
- They are unable to recognise that other people may have 'their own' representation of the world in their heads.
- Suggests ToM is an innate human capability, which unfolds as the child matures.

Strengths
- Standardised procedure – replicable.
- Controls by using the naming, memory and reality questions – results are not due to misunderstandings or memory problems.
- Controls by using Down syndrome children – results are not due to general intellectual ability.
- Controls by using preschool children – results are not due to lack of development.

Weaknesses
- Artificial setting may lead to demand characteristics.
- Low ecological validity – autistic children are known not to engage in 'pretend' play.
- Reductionist – focuses on information processing and ignores complexities of human life; emotions, social influences, physiological processes.

Alternative
Field experiment; use observations in child's own home with parents hiding Dad's glasses and asking child where Dad will look for them.

✔ Increased ecological validity and less prone to demand characteristics.

✘ Less control over the procedure.

Applications
- Effective treatment.
- Changing people's attitudes and beliefs.

Quick test

1. *How many solutions would a convergent thinker look for in a problem?*
2. *What is a schema?*
3. *What are the two main types of reasoning?*
4. *Why did Baron-Cohen use Down syndrome children?*
5. *What is the critical question in the Sally-Anne test and why?*
6. *What are the major impairments of an autistic child?*

1. One best solution. 2. A block of knowledge. 3. Inductive and deductive. 4. As a control – to show results could not be due to general intellectual ability. 5. The belief question – the ability to attribute beliefs to others (ToM). 6. Difficulties with social interaction and communication and repetitive and stereotyped patterns of behaviour.

Language

The distinction between words and language is very important.

- **The way words are combined turns them into a language. The rules of combination are called a 'grammar'.**

So is the distinction between language and communication.

- **Everyone agrees that animals can communicate with each other; the disagreement is whether they use something similar to human language to do this.**

Theories of language

Nature – the nativist theory (Noam Chomsky)

- Children are born with an **innate Language Acquisition Device** (LAD).
- The ability to use language is hard-wired into the brain – we are 'prepared' to learn language and all children acquire language in similar stages.
- Emphasises the difference between performance (using) and competence (understanding).

Nurture – the behaviourist theory (B. F. Skinner)

- Children learn by **imitation** and **reinforcement**.
- They imitate what they hear and are reinforced when correct.
- Gradually vocalisations are shaped and words are learned.
- Emphasises performance.

The language–thought relationship

Sapir-Whorf hypothesis (1956)

An individual's thoughts are determined by the categories made available to them by their language.

Piaget's developmental approach

Cognitive development is required before linguistic development is possible.

Children who do not conserve do not use relative terms (e.g. bigger) – Sinclair-de-Zwart (1969).

Vygotsky's developmental approach

Language and thought initially develop independently of each other and merge at about 2 years, when language begins to shape more complex thought.

Acquiring a new word is just the beginning of the development of a concept.

Comparison of language

Human language and communication in other species

Gardner and Gardner tried to teach sign language to a chimpanzee (Washoe). If Washoe could be shown to have learned language then it would provide support for Skinner's theory of behaviourism.

Terrace 1979 (chimp named Nim Chimpsky) criticised Washoe study. Difference between children and Nim (and Washoe):

- No increase in length of sentences in chimps.
- Increase in imitation in chimps that gradually decreases in children.
- Only 12% of Nim's utterances were spontaneous but much more of children's talk is unprompted.
- Nim (and Washoe) never learned to 'take turns' when talking – never learned the rules of the 'language game'.

Savage-Rumbaugh (1980s) – Lana, Austin and Sherman and Kanzi were taught to use a 'lexigram'.

- Kanzi showed quite impressive linguistic skills including learning the rule 'action precedes object' (which Washoe did not grasp).

Teaching sign language to a chimpanzee – Gardner and Gardner (Washoe) 1969

Aim
Can language be taught to a chimpanzee?

Participant
A female chimp, Washoe, aged approximately 1 year.

Method
- Case study – American Sign Language (ASL) was used without additional 'finger spelling'.
- Washoe lived in caravan in garden of the Gardner's.
- Instrumental learning – tickling most effective reward.
- More natural form of teaching – bringing something to her attention and making an appropriate sign (as with children).
- The dependent variable was measured by **observing**. A sign was assumed to be learned if Washoe spontaneously used it, it was seen by three observers and it was used over 15 days.

Results
First single words = come, gimme, hurry, sweet, tickle.

In the first 7 months Washoe learned 4 signs; in the next 7 months, 9 more and in the next 7 months, 21 more. After 22 months she had learned 30 signs and after 4 years she had learned 132.

Results summary – can WASHOE use language?
Displacement – yes.
Semanticity – yes, e.g. signed 'toothbrush' in bathroom.
Structure dependence – no, e.g. 'go sweet' or 'sweet go' both meant take me to the raspberry bushes.
Creativity – some, but limited, e.g. 'gimme tickle', 'open food drink'.
Generalisation – yes, e.g. 'more' – first used with tickle then generalised, e.g. food, drink, pushing in laundry basket.

Strengths
- Case study allows researchers to get to know the participant really well.
- Detailed and in-depth data collected.

Weaknesses
- Was Washoe responding to cues from her trainers?
- Is ASL truly a language?
- Observer bias and difficulty of recording signs promptly.

Ethical concerns
- Removed from home and family at a young age.
- Brought up in 'unnatural' environment.
- Informed consent and debriefing not appropriate for Washoe!

Conclusions
It seems possible to initiate simple communication with chimpanzees but they do not seem able to learn language in the same way as children.

Application
The Great Ape Project: an organisation proposing equal rights to the apes.

Criteria for language – Linguistic universals

- **Semanticity** – words have meanings.
- **Displacement** – the ability to use words to refer to things that are not present in time and space.
- **Structure dependence** – words can be 'chunked together' and moved around to make different meanings.
- **Creativity** – each sentence that is spoken could be a unique 'utterance'.
- **Generalisation** – from one situation to another.

Quick test

1. *What are the criteria for language?*
2. *What is a Language Acquisition Device (LAD)?*
3. *If Washoe had learned a language, why would this provide support for Skinner?*
4. *What is the difference between Piaget's and Vygotsky's views of thinking and language?*
5. *Which of the criteria for language did Washoe not manage?*

1. Semanticity, displacement, structure dependence, creativity, generalisation. 2. The brain is hard-wired with the ability to acquire language through different stages of development. 3. Behaviourist theory suggests that language can be learned through reinforcement. 4. Piaget suggests cognition is required before language; Vygotsky suggests they develop independently and merge at age 2 years. 5. Structure dependence.

Practice questions

Use these to test your progress. Check your answers on pages 92–95.

Cognitive psychology

1 What is meant by the term 'encoding'? [2]

....

2 Why are rhyming letters harder to recall than non-rhyming letters? [2]

....

3 What is the capacity of short-term memory? [2]

....

4 What is meant by the term 'declarative knowledge'? [2]

....

5 What is the main criticism of the multi-store model of memory? [2]

....

6 What controls memory in the 'working memory model'? [2]

....

7 How can memory be improved according to the levels of processing model? [2]

....

8 What is the difference between forgetting in STM and forgetting in LTM? [2]

....

9 What is meant by the term 'displacement'? [2]

....

10 What is meant by the term 'retroactive interference'? [2]

....

11 What is the main criticism of memory studies? [2]

....

12 What is the role of context in memory? [2]

....

13 What is meant by the term 'flashbulb' memory? [2]

....

14 Evaluate the research into eye witness testimony. [6]

....

....

....

....

....

15 Is our perception due to nature or nurture? [2]

....

....

16 What is the difference between Broadbent's filter model of attention and Triesman's attenuation model? [2]

....

....

17 Why could the Africans not say which animal was being speared in Hudson's 'antelope and elephant picture'? [2]

....

18 What are 'imposed etics'? [2]

....

....

19 What are the criteria for language? [2]

....

20 What is the nativist theory of language? [2]

....

21 What were the main differences found between children learning a language and the performance of chimpanzees? [2]

....

....

22 What are the ethical objections to the Gardners' study of Washoe? [2]

....

23 What training methods did the Gardners use to teach Washoe language? [2]

....

24 Can Washoe use language? [2]

....

....

25 What is meant by the term 'theory of mind'? [2]

....

Total /54

Development of attachments

Developmental psychology attempts to explain behaviour in terms of the ways in which people change as they age. Changes may be due to inherited factors (nature) or to the influence of other people and the physical environment (nurture).

Attachment

A long-lasting, close and strong bond between two people, shown by:

- a desire to maintain proximity and general orientation towards an attachment figure;
- distress on separation;
- pleasure on reunion.

Bowlby's theory of attachment (1969)

Imprinting

The tendency of birds to follow the first moving object they see after hatching (Lorenz). This natural instinct is an adaptive behaviour that aids survival. Bowlby suggests that something similar happens in humans.

- **Monotropy** – suggests infants are genetically programmed to form attachments to a single caregiver – important for healthy emotional development.
- **Critical period** – attachment with main caregiver occurs within a critical or sensitive period (approximately 2½ years) – not possible after this.
- **Criticism** – may not be a natural instinct but could be a kind of learning that takes place most easily during a certain stage of development – a sensitive rather than a critical period.

Skin-to-skin hypothesis

Hormones released by mother and infant in the first few days after birth help attachments to develop most easily (Klaus and Kennell 1976).

- Some support; however, early experience is no longer considered vital – attachment can develop over time.

Schaffer and Emerson's theory of attachment (1964)

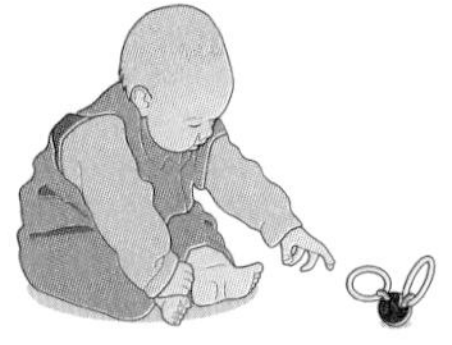

Longitudinal study (2 years) in working class area of Glasgow. Observations of 60 infants aged between 5 weeks and 18 months.

Findings

Attachment appears to develop in three stages:

- Up to 3 months – pre-attachment stage or asocial – no behaviour directed at any given individual.
- 3–7 months – indiscriminate attachment stage – attachment-seeking behaviour directed at numerous people.
- 7–9 months – specific attachments to one individual – both separation and stranger anxiety shown.

Evaluation

- Direct observation – observer bias and expectation effects.
- Records kept by mothers – relies on memory and accuracy of reports.
- More ecologically valid than artificial lab studies such as Strange Situation.
- Biased sample – one place, one social class.
- Very young infants are asocial, and incapable of distinguishing between different caregivers.

Carpenter (1975)

- Babies as young as 2 weeks can recognise their mother's face and voice.
- When shown pictures of mother and of a stranger, most infants looked at mother for a longer period.
- Became distressed when shown picture of mother but heard a stranger's voice.

Multiple attachments

In opposition to Bowlby's theory, Schaffer suggests that **multiple** attachments can be formed within a **'sensitive time period'**.

Individual differences in attachment

'Strange Situation' test (SS) devised by Mary Ainsworth 1971.

Types of attachment

Secure attachment (Type B): child is distressed at mother leaving and easily comforted upon her return.

Insecure attachment (three types):

- **Anxious–resistant** (Type C): child is discontented with mother, distressed at mother leaving and later resists contact.
- **Anxious–avoidant** (Type A): child ignores mother; is not affected by her parting or return and is easily comforted by strangers.
- **Disorganised** (added later by Main and Solomon 1986): child lacks coping strategies for SS and often uses a chaotic mix of approach and avoidance.

Reliability of SS

- If the same child is tested at various times, the same result is achieved.

Validity of SS

- Criterion validity – use a set criterion, perhaps from another test.
- May not be measuring innate personality but different relationships – child could have other or more important attachment figures than the mother.
- A **strange** situation! It is carried out in a laboratory and therefore lacks ecological validity.

Discussion

These differences in attachment may be due to:

- **Parental sensitivity** – quality (responsiveness) rather than quantity (time or feeding) is most important.
- **Infant temperament** – e.g. Kagan 1982 suggests that innate differences in infant temperament and anxiety may cause certain kinds of parental reaction and attachment.
- **Family circumstances** – attachment type may vary over time and setting with social and cultural environmental conditions, e.g. stressful periods (e.g. Vaughn et al. 1979).

Cross-cultural studies

These find general agreement of the classification of attachment types.

- Majority of children in most cultures are securely attached.
- Higher proportion of German children insecure rather than secure; of these, higher proportion of avoidant and very few resistant.
- Insecure Israeli children – higher proportion of resistant and very few avoidant.

Explanations:

- Multiple attachments are found in some cultures and subcultures.
- Israeli infants are mainly raised communally in large groups.
- German culture fosters independence in children from a very early age.

Criticisms:

- The SS may not be universally valid: based upon American cultural assumptions.
- Imposed ethics – same behaviour may mean something different in different cultures, e.g. separation in Japan is virtually unknown to infants.
- Van Ijzendoorn and Kroonenberg (1988) – variation within cultures is far greater than variation across cultures.

Quick test

1. *What is 'monotropy'?*
2. *Who disagrees with Bowlby's idea of the 'critical period'?*
3. *When are children 'asocial' and what does this mean?*
4. *In Ainsworth's Strange Situation, how did insecure avoidant children behave?*
5. *How can the validity of the Strange Situation be measured?*
6. *What explanation is there for the fact that a high proportion of insecure German children were anxious-avoidant?*

1. Infants are genetically programmed to form attachments to a **single** caregiver. 2. Schaffer and Emerson suggest that multiple attachments are formed during a more 'sensitive time period'. 3. Up to 3 months – pre-attachment stage with no behaviour directed at any given individual. 4. Infant ignores mother (avoidant) and is easily comforted by strangers. 5. By using criterion validity, i.e. a child measured as secure using SS should also be measured as emotionally healthy and socially adjusted at later ages. 6. German culture fosters independence in children from a very early age.

Explanations of attachment

These should explain why attachments form in the first place as well as how this happens. They should also reliably account for the findings of relevant research studies. Attachment behaviour may be due to:

- nature – Bowlby's theory;
- nurture – learning theory;
- interaction between the two – Freud's theory.

Bowlby's theory

This suggests that attachment is:

- **Adaptive** – attachments are adaptive in that they aid survival.
  - The primary attachment relationship (monotropy) creates proximity-seeking behaviour – this brings with it food, security and a safe base from which to explore the world.
  - Later attachments are based on the 'internal working model' (IWM) – a cognitive schema representing this first relationship.
- **Innate** – a natural instinct (due to nature).
- **Reciprocal** – attachments depend upon interactions, not simply on time spent together.

Bowlby = A.I.R.

- **For the parent**, attachment ensures a greater likelihood of their offspring surviving and thus passing on their own genes.
- Innate social releasers such as crying and smiling are a fundamental part of the attachment process.

Evidence for the IWM

Hazan and Shaver 1987, from self-reports on a questionnaire returned via a newspaper advert, found that

- Experiences of attachment in infancy influence styles of love relationships in adulthood.
- Securely attached infants experienced happy and trusting relationships and anxious-avoidant infants avoided intimacy in adult relationships.

Evidence against the IWM

- **Jacobson and Wille 1986**: positive correlations may be explained by the innate temperament of the child. If a child is predisposed to form happy, healthy relationships then this would explain both their early experiences and their adult relationships.
- **Main and Weston 1981** found only very low correlations among children's different relationships.

Evaluation of studies into IWM

- Data relies heavily on retrospective self-reports; unreliable memories plus socially desirability effects.
- IWM relies on idea of monotropy and for many cultures multiple attachments seem to be the norm – Schaffer and Emerson 1964.

Learning theories – behaviourism

Classical conditioning

Learning occurs through making a link between two different stimuli.

Unconditioned stimulus...food	→	Unconditioned reflex... sense of pleasure
Neutral stimulus...mother	→	No response
NS (mother) paired with UCS (food)	→	NS now becomes conditioned stimulus and produces a conditioned response...sense of pleasure

Operant conditioning

Learning occurs through making a link between behaviour and its consequences.

- Any behaviour that is rewarded is more likely to be repeated.
- Mother (secondary reinforcer) provides food (primary reinforcer) for infant, reducing its primary drive of hunger.

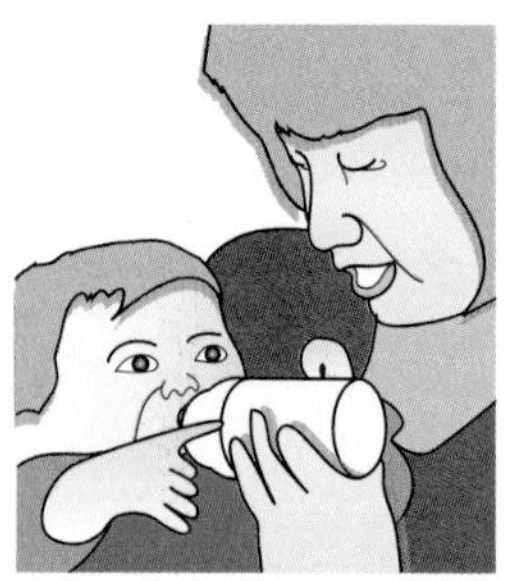

Evaluation of learning theories

- **Harlow's** study with monkeys demonstrates how food alone is not enough for attachments to form (bearing in mind generalisability of animal studies to humans).
- **Schaffer and Emerson 1964** – 40% of human infants were most attached to an adult who did not feed and bathe them, but who was most responsive to them – quality rather than quantity.
- Learning explanations are reductionist – simple 'stimulus-response' reinforcements.

Behaviourism continued

Harry Harlow 1959

Very young rhesus monkeys were removed from their mothers and placed in cages with two 'substitute' mothers, one made of wire mesh and the other covered in cloth.

- Most infants spent longer on the cloth mother, even if it did not provide food.
- When frightened by a toy drummer, the infants ran to the cloth monkey for comfort.
- The monkeys grew up with many problems, particularly when interacting with others.

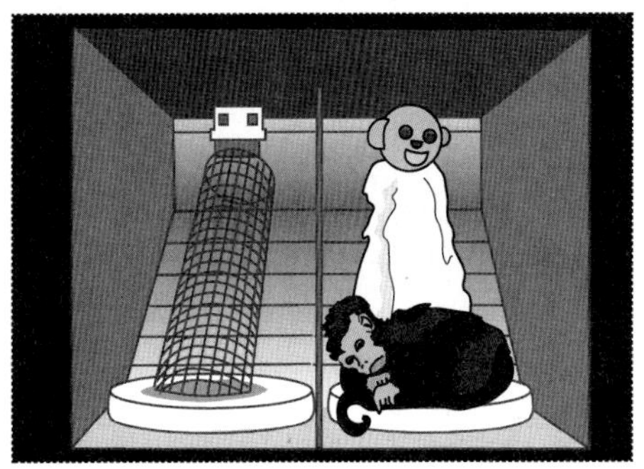

Criticisms:

- Unethical and would not be allowed today.
- Confounding variables – not just maternal deprivation; monkeys also deprived of social interaction.

Social learning theory

Suggests that attachment, and relationships generally, are learned through imitation plus some mental processing (see Core Study, page 43). **Hay and Vespo 1988** suggest that attachment is learned because it is reinforced. Learning takes place through:

- **Modelling**: imitation of parent's behaviour.
- **Vicarious reinforcement**: learn by watching others, seeing the rewards they receive and then imitating them.
- **Direct instruction**: parents teach children explicitly how to behave in an affectionate way.
- **Social facilitation**: encouraging behaviour through helpful assistance.

Evaluation of social learning theory

Some attachment behaviour has been shown to be due to the above processes; however, this does not explain the intense emotional bond often shown in parent–child relationships.

The psychodynamic approach

- Freud's theory of personality development relies heavily on the experiences of early infancy and the interaction between biological drive (id = pleasure) and social environment (usually mother) (see Core Study, page 42).
- An infant becomes attached to its mother because she gives it pleasure through feeding. This is sometimes described as 'cupboard love'. The mother is the first love-object.

Evaluation of the psychodynamic approach

- As with learning theory, evidence suggests feeding alone is not enough to form strong attachments.
- No empirical evidence for Freud's theories.

EXAMINER'S TOP TIP

Weigh up the strengths and limitations of each explanation.

Quick test

1. *According to Bowlby, what is attachment?*
2. *How is attachment behaviour adaptive?*
3. *What is an 'internal working model'?*
4. *Is there any evidence for the IWM?*
5. *What evidence is there against the idea that attachment is learned through reinforcement through feeding?*
6. *What is vicarious reinforcement?*

1. Bowlby's theory says that attachment is AIR = adaptive, innate and reciprocal. 2. It aids survival; proximity-seeking behaviour brings food and safety and the development of an internal working model of relationships. 3. A cognitive schema representing the first relationship. This is used as a prototype for all other relationships. 4. Yes. Hazan and Shaver 1987 showed how securely attached infants experienced happy relationships in adulthood. 5. Harlow's study with monkeys demonstrates how food alone is not enough for attachments to form. 6. Learning by watching others, seeing the rewards they receive, then imitating that behaviour.

Deprivation and privation

Deprivation is the lack of a major attachment figure during the critical period of attachment (2–3 years of age).

Short-term effects of deprivation

Robertson's famous film of hospitalised children presented observations of 1- to 4-year-olds separated from the primary caregiver for short periods.

Findings

Symptoms of the **'syndrome of distress'**: PDD model.

- **P**rotest: cries a lot and expresses anger, fear and frustration.
- **D**espair: shows signs of depression, apathy and avoidance.
- **D**etachment: interacts with others but only on a superficial level and shows no preference.

Re-attachment is avoided and resisted – may cause a delay in intellectual development.

Evaluation

- Effects may be due to factors concerning the hospital environment rather than separation itself.
- Does not take individual differences into account.

Long-term effects of deprivation

Maternal deprivation hypothesis – Bowlby 1953

A break in the bond during the early years will have serious and irreversible effects on the cognitive, emotional and social development of the child.

Forty-four thieves – Bowlby 1946

Studied 44 children referred to a child guidance clinic because of stealing; 32% showed affectionless psychopathy – a disorder involving a lack of guilt and remorse.

- 86% of these had experienced separation of at least 1 week before the age of 5 years.
- Only 17% of those not diagnosed with affectionless psychopathy had experienced such separation.

Evaluation

- Correlations do not identify cause and effect.
- Many separations had been for very short periods.
- Retrospective information about the separation.
- Researcher expectations – Bowlby diagnosed the condition himself.

Deprivation dwarfism

Poor physical outcome from institutional care may be due to physical deprivation, although Widdowson 1951 found that:

- an improved diet in orphaned children did not lead to weight gain, but
- a more sympathetic and responsive supervisor did.

Suggests that emotional deprivation may be more harmful than physical deprivation.

Anaclitic depression

Loss of appetite and a sense of resigned helplessness. Children in orphanages and institutions in South America (Spitz 1945) showed a particular form of depression: apathy, helplessness and lack of appetite.

Individual differences and deprivation

Characteristics of the child

- Temperament – e.g. an aggressive child may become more aggressive whilst a shy child may become shyer.
- Age – Maccoby 1981 suggests that between 7 months and 3 years is an especially vulnerable stage.
- Gender – on average, boys tend to respond more negatively than girls.

Previous experience

- Type of attachment with parent pre-separation (e.g. secure/insecure) – Barrett 1977.
- Previous experience of separation (e.g. history of day-care).
- Attachment to others (Schaffer and Emerson suggest multiple attachments is the 'norm').
- Quality of care given in the hospital.

Research into effects of privation

Privation occurs when a child has never formed a close bond with anyone: this is perhaps more serious for the child than deprivation. Rutter suggests that effects found by Bowlby were due to privation rather than deprivation, and that privation may have more permanent consequences.

Rutter's Isle of Wight study 1976

- Over 2 000 boys – delinquency correlated with psychiatric illness in the caregivers or discord within the family.
- No delinquency found when separation was due to other reasons, e.g. physical illness or death of the mother.

Case study of Genie – Curtiss 1977

- Genie was found in 1970, aged 13, having spent most of the time locked in a room.
- She could not stand straight, speak or understand language, or socialise.
- Many cognitive skills improved: however, language and social skills were permanently underdeveloped.

Reactive attachment disorder

Described in DSM-IV. RAD is probably due to lack of responsiveness from major caregiver in early years and appears to have permanent effects.

- Lack of trust.
- Overly self-dependent.
- Lack of conscience.
- Over-controlling of others and ignore their needs – steal, damage and destroy anything outside of their own control.

Reversibility of privation effects

Evidence of reversibility

Adoption studies

Hodges and Tizard 1989 (see Core Study, page 42).

Case studies of extreme privation – Freud and Dann 1951

- Studied six 3-year-old orphans who had spent time in a concentration camp.
- Formed close attachments to each other and did not develop affectionless psychopathy.
- Intellectual recovery, however emotional problems in later life were difficult to overcome.

Isolated rhesus monkeys – Novak and Harlow 1975

- Socially isolated monkeys developed near-normally if they were given 'therapy' later by being allowed to play with monkeys of their own age.
- Generalising from animals to humans is difficult.

EXAMINER'S TOP TIP

Make sure you can discuss the difference between deprivation and privation, and back up your statements with evidence.

Quick test

1. ***What is the difference between deprivation and privation?***
2. ***What is the final stage of the PDD model?***
3. ***What is affectionless psychopathy and who discovered it?***
4. ***Why is the case study of Genie (Curtiss 1977) unreliable?***
5. ***What is 'reactive attachment disorder'?***
6. ***Why did the orphans from the concentration camp not develop affectionless psychopathy?***

1. Deprivation occurs when a bond or attachment is broken; privation occurs when an attachment has never been formed.
2. Detachment: infant interacts with others but only on a superficial level and shows no preference. 3. Disorder involving a lack of guilt and remorse. Bowlby diagnosed 32% of his '44 thieves' as having it. 4. Subjective interpretation of findings and researcher bias.
5. A disorder described in DSM-IV: sufferers lack trust, are overly self-dependent, lack conscience and are over-controlling of others.
6. They made attachments to each other.

Institutionalisation and aggression

This spread covers two investigations:

- **Social and family relationships of ex-institutional adolescents (Hodges and Tizard 1989).**
- **Transmission of aggression through imitation of aggressive models – Bobo Doll Study (Bandura, Ross and Ross 1961).**

Hodges and Tizard 1989

Aim

To investigate whether experiencing early institutionalisation will lead to long-term problems for adolescents.

Method

- Longitudinal study (children at 4, 8 and 16 years); this study focuses on age 16.
- Institution policy insisted that carers did not form attachments to children. By 4 years the children had, on average, 50 carers.
- Participants: 39 children aged 16, placed in an institution when they were less than 4 months old.
- At age 16, 39 children were interviewed: 23 adopted, 11 restored to family and 5 remaining in institution.
- **Independent variable (I/V)**: the environment of the participant – ex-institutional (**adopted** or **restored**), control group 1 (matched for age, sex, position in family, one- or two-parent family) and control group 2 (school friend matched for age and sex).
- **Dependent variable (D/V)**: responses to questionnaires and assessments of social relationships with family, peers and teachers.
- Data collected by:
  - interview with participant – Questionnaire of Social Difficulty (Linsay 1982);
  - interview with mother or care-worker – 'A' scale questionnaire (Rutter et al. 1970);
  - questionnaire to teachers – Rutter 'B' scale.

Results

	Ex-institutional children	
Family relationships	Adopted	Restored
Attachments to parents	As attached as control	Less attached than control group and adopted group
Relationships with siblings	More problems than control group	More problems than control group and adopted
Showing affection	More affectionate than restored	Less affectionate than control group
Confiding and support	No difference	No difference
Relationships with peers	Worse than control	Worse than control

Conclusion

- Children deprived of close and lasting attachments to adults in their first years can make such attachments later on **but** this depends on how adults nurture these attachments.
- Institutionalised children show long-term differences and difficulties in social relationships, not related to family type.

Applications

Care within institutions and precautions against long-term affects of care – relates to hospitalisation of children, children's homes or foster care and adoption.

Strengths

- Ecological validity.
- Quantitative data statistically analysed.
- Qualitative data provides in-depth data involving subjective feelings of participants.

Weaknesses

Qualitative data difficult to analyse.

- Self-reports may lack reliability; e.g. social desirability or experimenter expectations.
- Lack of validity of questionnaires – measuring 'social difficulty'?
- Lack of control in natural experiments – randomly assigned to groups and therefore does not take individual differences into account.
- Attrition of sample – participants dropping out of longitudinal study.
- Ethical issues – asking questions that may disrupt interpersonal relationships, e.g. asking mothers if they loved all their children equally; asking participant if they have a special friend.

Alternative

Observations of behaviour in real-life family settings – increase ecological validity.

EXAMINER'S TOP TIP

Procedure, findings and conclusions can all be asked for in exam questions.

Bandura, Ross and Ross 1961

Aim

To demonstrate that aggressive behaviour is learned through observation of a model and that imitation can occur in the absence of that model (social learning theory).

Method

Laboratory experiment.

Three conditions (aggressive model, non-aggressive model, no model) – 12 boys and 12 girls in each condition.

Matched pairs design – matched for levels of aggression.

Participants: 36 boys and 36 girls (age range 3–5 years).

I/V: Level 1 – aggressive or non-aggressive role model; Level 2 – same-sex or opposite-sex role model.

Procedure

Phase one – modelling the behaviour phase

- The non-aggressive model played with the toys in a quiet manner.
- The aggressive model made specific acts of aggression toward the Bobo doll; sitting on it, punching on nose, kicking it and saying 'POW' or 'He sure is a tough fellow'.

Phase two – arousal

- Shown toys they were not allowed to play with in order to provoke the children and to ensure that the non-aggressive group was given an equal chance at showing aggression.

Phase three – observation

- Taken to another room containing toys, including 3ft Bobo doll, guns, etc.

Results

Children in aggressive condition:

- imitated many modelled physical and verbal aggressive behaviours (and non-aggressive behaviours);
- displayed **much** more non-imitative aggressive behaviour.

Children in non-aggressive condition:

- imitated very few of the modelled behaviours;
- spent more time playing with toys and doing nothing.

Boys imitated more physical aggression (but not verbal). Evidence of 'same-sex' effect.

Conclusion

- Learning can take place by observation without conditioning.
- Children are more likely to learn from same-sex models.
- Freud's theory of 'identification' may be used to explain learning.

Strengths

- Controlled manipulation of conditions and use of control group.
- Matched pairs design.

Weaknesses

- Observer bias.
- Unstandardised presentation of behaviour – later experiments used video presentation.
- Lack of ecological validity – Liebert and Baron (1972) used real TV programmes and willingness to hurt another child.
- Demand characteristics – children may have believed they should behave aggressively; no restraints on aggressive behaviour.

Ethical issues

- Distress caused to children.
- Informed consent from parents, not children.
- Debriefing – may not understand.
- 'Teaching' children to be aggressive.

Applications

Children learning aggressive behaviour from watching violence on TV – 9pm watershed.

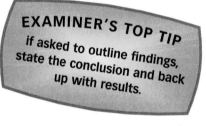

EXAMINER'S TOP TIP

if asked to outline findings, state the conclusion and back up with results.

Quick test

1. Which group of children were 'least attached' and why?
2. How were the children's attachments and peer relationships measured?
3. What are the limitations of this way of measuring?
4. Why did Bandura use a 'matched pairs' design?
5. Sum up Bandura's conclusion.

1. Restored were least attached – attachments appear to depend on adults concerned and how much they nurture such attachments. 2. Interviews and questionnaires with participant, mother/caregiver and teacher. 3. Reliability (consistency of measuring), validity (measuring what you think), social desirability (saying what you think you should), demand characteristics. 4. To ensure equal levels of aggression before the experiment. 5. Learning can take place by observation without any operant conditioning.

Personality and conservation

This spread covers two investigations:

- **Analysis of a phobia in a five-year old boy (Freud 1909).**
- **Asking only one question in the conservation experiment (Samuel and Bryant 1984).**

Freud 1909

Aim

A case study of 'Little Hans' to provide support for his psychoanalytic theory.

1. The unconscious nature of our drives and motivations

The biological id wants to gain pleasure from meeting instinctual needs (eat, sleep, eliminate) whilst the superego internalises the rules of society (from parents), putting limits on the id's desires. The ego must please id without upsetting superego, by using **defence mechanisms**, e.g.:

- **Displacement** – redirect feelings onto another target. Freud – phobias are caused by unconscious anxiety being displaced onto external objects.
- **Denial** – completely reject thoughts or feelings.
- **Suppression** – vaguely aware of thought or feeling but try to hide it.
- **Projection** – think someone else has your thought or feeling.

2. The five psychosexual stages of development

- **Oral** (birth–1 year) – id is in control – pleasure sought through the mouth (e.g. sucking).
- **Anal** (1–3 years) – ego develops – elimination of faeces is the source of pleasure.
- **Phallic** (3–5/6 years) – superego develops – driven by the anxiety principle: Oedipus conflict (boys) – young boys direct their drive for sexual pleasure (libido) onto their mothers and fear their father as he may find out; Electra conflict (girls) – opposite effect towards father and mother.
- **Latent** (6–puberty) – no unconscious conflicts.
- **Genital** (adulthood) – re-emergence of earlier drives; forming loving relationships.

Method

Case study. Psychoanalytic analysis carried out by correspondence and interviews with Hans' father and with Hans himself over a number of years between the ages of 3 and 5 (Freud's 'phallic stage').

Results of Freud's analysis

Behaviour of Hans	Freud's explanation	Freud's conclusion
Asking mother to powder his penis	An attempt to seduce his mother	Oedipus complex
Fear of bath	Death wish against sister as attention given to her	Oedipus complex
Dream of taking small giraffe away from large giraffe	Desire to take mother away from father	Oedipus complex
Fear of heavily loaded carts	Fear of another birth due to jealousy over mother's attention	Oedipus complex
Fear of being bitten by horses	Displacement of fear of father onto the horse	Fear of castration by father
Fantasy of plumber providing larger widdler	Identifying with his father and wanting to be like him	Resolution of Oedipus complex
Fantasy of being a father with his mother	Father delegated to grandfather as opposed to wanting him dead	Resolution of Oedipus complex

Conclusions drawn by Freud

- Support for his theory of sexuality and Oedipus complex.
- The nature of phobias; hidden conflicts of the unconscious mind (displacement).
- No searching through 'past memory'.

Strengths

- Freud dealt with real people and their problems.
- good 'ecological validity'.

Weaknesses

- Hans is analysed by his father who is emotionally involved and believes in Freud.
- Father 'put words into Hans' mouth'.
- 'Action research' – both scientific evidence and treatment. Should be separated because 'treating' what is being investigated may change it.
- Unscientific – subjective and irrefutable (can't be proven right or wrong), non-replicable.

Ethical issues

Treatment not very child-friendly (and included leading questions).

At age 19 Hans had no recollection of any of the discussions – 'no long-term effects'.

Samuel and Bryant 1984

Aim

To demonstrate that **asking the same question twice** causes children to make errors in the standard conservation test (conserving = understanding that quantity does not change when appearance changes).

Method

Participants: 252 boys and girls (from Devon) aged 5 to 8.5 years.

Stratified sample:

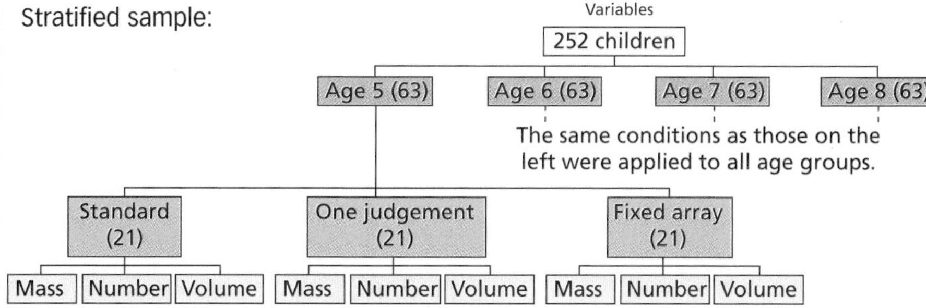

I/V: Level 1 (natural) – age; Level 2 (condition) – type of task; Level 3 (type of conservation).

All age groups given the same conditions:

- Standard group: traditional conservation task – asked two questions.
- One-judgement group: only one question asked, **after** the transformation.
- Fixed array group: saw only **one** display – the post-transformation one.

Asked: "is there the same amount in each or does one have more than the other?".

Procedure: Each child given 12 separate trials to test conservation of mass, volume and number: 2 equal and 2 unequal masses (plasticine); 2 x 2 numbers (counters) and 2 x 2 volumes (liquid). The numbers of errors were recorded.

Results

	Mean errors for each group		
Age	**Standard**	**1 judgement**	**Fixed array**
5	8	7	9
6	6	4	6
7	3	3	5
8	2	1	3

- Each age group made fewer errors than all younger age groups.
- One-judgement task significantly easier than other two tasks.
- Horizontal décalage = conservation of number easiest, then mass, then volume.

Conclusions

- Support for Piaget – ability to conserve increases with age.
- Challenge against Piaget – fewer errors if the procedure is changed slightly. Even young children can conserve. The repeated question generated **demand characteristics**.

Strengths

- 'Clinical interview' – flexibility.
- Quantitative data – easy to analyse.

Weaknesses

- Self-reports from children can be unreliable.
- Lack of ecological validity.
- Biased sample.
- Experimenter bias.

Ethical issues

- Informed consent from parent not child.
- Protection of children may be more difficult.
- Emotional distress – may believe they have got the question wrong.
- Debriefing – child may not understand.

Quick test

1. *Why does the ego develop defence mechanisms?*
2. *What defence mechanism had Little Hans developed?*
3. *Why is Freud's study unscientific?*
4. *What two things increased the possibility of children being able to conserve?*
5. *Why does this challenge Piaget's findings?*

1. Satisfy our biological drives for pleasure (id) without upsetting our internalised moral values (superego) and to prevent this internal conflict entering our consciousness. 2. Displacement – redirected his fear of father onto horse. 3. Data is subjective interpretation, irrefutable and case study is non-replicable. 4. Age and type of task (i.e. one-judgement easier than standard two questions). 5. Children can conserve earlier than originally thought.

Day care

Positive effects

More stimulation, interaction and educational activities for children who would not otherwise receive them.

Burchinal, Lee and Ramey 1989:

- Found a positive correlation between pre-school day care and IQ levels upon entering school.
- Stimulation received in day-care settings can improve cognitive development.

Negative effects

Less verbal interaction, stimulation and exploration by the child due to lack of secure attachment figure as a base.

Tizard 1979:

- Conversations between mother and child more complex than between day carer and child.
- Carers need to divide attention between many children, leading to less cognitive stimulation.

Kagan et al. 1980:

- Set up own nursery with consistent high-quality day care.
- Found no significantly consistent differences between day-care infants and matched home-care control group in attachment and sociability or cognitive development.

Cognitive effects seem to depend upon the quality of day care relative to care that the child would otherwise have received.

Operation Headstart

In the 1960s the USA gave several hundred thousand socially disadvantaged pre-school children intensive day-care education. Benefits: raised achievement at school in short term and social benefits in long term.

Where the quality of day care is low, children may not thrive.

Broberg et al. 1997:

- Studied 146 Swedish children assessed at aged 8.
- Day-care children performed better on verbal and mathematical tasks.
- Home-care children showed average performance.
- Childminded children performed worst.

Andersson 1992:

- Longitudinal study on 100 Swedish children from a range of backgrounds.
- At ages 8 and 13 children assessed by teachers and given an IQ test.
- Findings: those who entered day care before age of 1 had better school performance than those with no day care (performed worst).
- Evaluation: confounding variables; day-care children also tended to come from higher socio-economic groups (richer parents).

Vandell and Corasaniti 1990:

- Conducted a similar study in Texas.
- Findings: opposite to Anderson – day-care children were rated by teachers as having poor peer relationships and emotional health.
- Evaluation*:* quality of care more important than quantity of care; Sweden has higher standards of day care than Texas; Sweden has greater parental leave allowance – enables stronger attachments to be made before child enters day care.

Results from studies into day care are open to criticism

- Assessment of emotional, social and cognitive effects of day care depends on validity of tests used.
- **Strange Situation** often used; validity is questionable and may be culturally specific.
- Various IQ tests used to test for cognitive performances – questions over validity and reliability.
- Correlations do not identify cause and effect.

EXAMINER'S TOP TIP

Weigh up the benefits and disadvantages of day care for cognitive and social development.

The effects on children's social development

Positive effects

Increased sociability and social skills, more playful, outgoing and less aggressive due to greater exposure to the outside world.

Clarke-Stewart, Gruber and Fitzgerald 1994:

- 150 children aged between 2 and 3, in Chicago day care.
- Peer relationships more advanced in day-care children.
- Equal amounts of distress in the Strange Situation for 30 hours or 10 hours of day care.

Negative effects

- Child unable to form an attachment (causing privation effects) or disruption to the bond if attachment already made (causing deprivation effects).

Belsky and Rovine 1988:

- Infants more likely to develop insecure attachments if they received day care for over 20 hours per week before they were a year old.

Individual differences

Some children benefit whilst others do not.

Egeland and Hiester 1995:

- Child's pre-existing characteristics.
- 70 children from poor backgrounds – half home care and half day care.
- In the Strange Situation, day care appeared to have negative effects on secure children but positive effects on insecure children.

The National Institute of Child Health and Human Development (NICHD):

- Maternal sensitivity.
- Study of Early Childcare (1997) – 1 000 mothers and their infants aged 6 months and again at 15 months.
- No difference in emotional adjustment.
- Mothers low in responsiveness were more likely to have children with insecure attachments if they also experienced poor day care.

Improving the quality of day care

More consistent care

- 'Key workers' are now common to avoid many different carers.
- Staff turnover should be kept to a minimum by looking after them too.

Better interactions with infants

- High staff to child ratios will enable more complex verbal interactions to occur (Tizard 1979).

More stimulating environments

- Availability of age-appropriate play equipment, books and outdoor space are important for cognitive development.

More sensitive care

- In-service training should be provided to improve responsiveness of carers.

Effects of day-care separation on parents

- Bond disruption should be minimised – need good links between home and day care.
- If mothers are happy with day care, may feel less depressed and able to provide higher quality of care when they are with their children.

Quick test

1. ***How was Kagan sure that consistent, high-quality day care had the same effects as good home care?***
2. ***Which children are more at risk from the negative effects of day care?***
3. ***Who found that 20 hours of day care a week was likely to lead infants to develop insecure attachments?***
4. ***How is consistency in day care accomplished?***
5. ***What are the main criticisms of studies into day care?***

1. Used a matched home-care control group. 2. Socially disadvantaged children (Headstart), securely attached (Egeland and Hiester) or children whose mothers are low in responsiveness (NICHD). 3. Belsky and Rovine 1988. 4. High standards = low staff turnover, use of 'key workers' and in-service training. 5. Validity of tests (IQ and SS) and suggestions of causality from correlations.

Practice questions

Use these to test your progress. Check your answers on pages 92–95.

Developmental psychology

1 What are the three stages of the development of attachment in Schaffer and Emerson's theory (1964)? [2]

....

2 What is meant by the term 'attachment'? [2]

....

3 What individual differences are there in attachments? [2]

....

4 What might individual differences in attachment be due to? [2]

....

5 Why is the 'Strange Situation' not universally valid? [2]

....

6 Why do parents form attachments to their babies? [2]

....

7 Why is the evidence for the 'internal working model' unreliable? [2]

....

8 How does social learning theory suggest that attachments are formed? [2]

....

9 Outline the short-term effects of deprivation. [2]

....

10 Describe Bowlby's maternal deprivation hypothesis. [2]

....

11 What is meant by the term 'anaclitic depression'? [2]

....

12 Evaluate Bowlby's '44 thieves' study. [3]

....

....

13 What is the difference between Bowlby and Rutter's explanations for maladjustment in children? [2]

....

14 Outline individual differences in how children respond to being deprived of an attachment figure. [2]

....

15 Outline the findings of Rutter's Isle of Wight study (1976). [2]

....

16 What is the conclusion drawn from the case study of Genie by Curtiss in 1977? [2]

....

17 Outline the evidence for the reversibility of privation effects. [2]

....

18 Can deprived children make attachments later in life? [2]

....

19 What conclusion did Bandura et al. reach in their study of aggression? [2]

....

20 According to Freud's psychoanalytic theory, is our personality due to nature or nurture? [2]

....

21 What evidence did Freud present in support of the Oedipus conflict? [2]

....

22 What ethical issues are raised when studying children? [2]

....

23 Outline the possible benefits of day care on children's cognitive development. [3]

....

....

24 Outline the possible negative effects of day care on children's social development. [3]

....

....

25 Evaluate the evidence for the effects of day care. [3]

....

....

Total /54

Conformity and minority influence

To conform is to follow group 'norms' – patterns of behaviour representative or typical of a group. It is possible for a minority to influence the behaviour of a group.

Research studies into majority influence

Conformity studies

Jenness 1932

- Students asked to estimate number of beans in a jar.
- After discussing guesses with group, individual estimates converged towards the group estimate.

Sherif 1935

- Autokinetic effect.
- Tested alone, participants developed their own norm for estimating strength and direction of movement of a spot of light.
- Tested in groups of three, judgements tended to be closer together.

Evaluation:

- Artificial situation – lacking ecological validity.
- Jacobs and Campbell 1961 – tested using all but one giving the same judgement: strong evidence of conformity.

Asch 1956

- Tested conformity using an unambiguous stimulus.

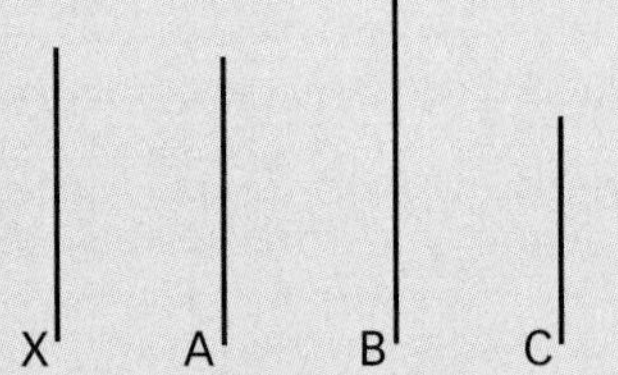

- A group of confederates agreed that line B matched line X.

Individual participants agreed with the group 37% of the time.

- Conformity effect increased when number of confederates rose from 1–3; no rise from 3–16.
- Presence of a supporter giving correct answer – conformity effect decreased to only 5%.

Evaluation:

- Culturally biased sample – Americans may be more conformist than others.
- Historical bias – people may have been more willing to conform in the 1950s.

Explanations for conformity

Informational social influence – Jennes and Sherif

We conform to gain information – likely to change private opinion.

Normative social influence

The desire to be liked by others – does not involve changing personal beliefs. Conformity can also be described in terms of:

- **Compliance** – superficially conforming in order to gain group acceptance.
- **Identification** – conforming to 'role' given by society in order to gain group membership, e.g. nurse.
- **Internalisation** – acceptance of group norms and change of private opinion.

Factors influencing conformity

Situational factors

- **Culture**: Smith and Bond 1993.
  - Historical: levels of conformity have steadily decreased since Asch's original study.
  - Ethnicity: in 20 cross-cultural studies, Indian teachers showed highest levels of conformity (58%), Belgian students the lowest (11%).
- **Deindividuation**: loss of a sense of personal identity.
  - Zimbardo 1969: Milgram-type experiment – participants all dressed alike. Levels of conforming to role of 'obedient participant' rose.
  - Johnson and Downing 1979: replicated this with nurses' uniforms – levels of obedience went down. Deindividuation influenced conformity to social roles.

Ed – no space to take line in second panel to a new line.

Dispositional (personality) factors

- **Personal control**: Burger and Cooper 1979 – people with high need for control were less likely to be influenced when rating cartoons.
- **Gender effects**: Eagly and Carli 1981 – women more conformist than men.

Non-conformity can be explained in terms of reactance. High need for personal control may lead individual to react against attempts to influence them – Venkatesan 1966.

Research studies into minority influence

Some people resist group pressure and follow minority opinion. Whilst individuals often *comply* with the majority, the minority can *convert* them, i.e. persuade the majority to agree with the minority.

Maass and Clark 1983

- Self-reports were used to measure attitudes to gay rights.
- Whilst private opinions were shifting towards the view of the minority, participants publicly expressed views demonstrated by the majority.

Moscovici et al. 1969

- Groups of six participants – shown slides varying in intensity of blue.
- Two confederates said ‘green’ on every trial: majority responded ‘green’ 8% of the time.
- Two confederates said ‘green’ on two thirds of trials: majority responded ‘green’ 1% of the time.

Kelley 1967 – attribution theory (see page 56)

- We try to decide whether other people’s behaviour is due to internal causes (personality) or external causes (social pressure).
- If behaviour of minority is **consistently** different from majority we may infer internal causes – **seriousness** and **sincerity** – may lead majority to question their own views.

Consistency is necessary, but not always sufficient on its own, for a minority to influence the majority.

Other likely conditions for conformity

- **Flexibility**: Nemeth, Swedlund and Kanki 1974 showed how rigidity and unrealistic responses in ‘blue-green slide’ study failed to achieve any conformity effects.
- **Commitment**: a committed minority can *convert* majority views.
- **Relevance** of minority arguments: social trends influence the relevance of arguments, which in turn influence levels of conformity.

Social impact theory

Can be used to explain both majority and minority influence. Social influence can be related to:

- **Strength**: number of people present and the number of times the opinions are expressed consistently.
- **Status**: a minority of one expert is of equal strength to a larger number of amateurs.
- **Immediacy**: physical proximity, e.g. face to face has more impact than reading. Psychological proximity, e.g. opinions of a friend are more influential than those of an acquaintance.

EXAMINER’S TOP TIP

You should be able to sum up the evidence for conformity and why some people resist.

Quick test

1. ***How did Sherif’s study demonstrate conformity?***
2. ***Why did Asch’s participants give an obviously wrong answer when judging line length?***
3. ***What is the main difference between majority and minority influence?***
4. ***Which type of social influence is likely to change private opinion?***
5. ***What type of minority influence is likely to change majority opinion?***
6. ***What are the main components of the theory which accounts for conformity and minority influence?***

1. When judging movement of light, judgements made in groups were closer together than if made alone. 2. Normative social influence: they wanted to be liked by others. 3. Individuals **comply** with the majority, and are **converted** by the minority. 4. Informational social influence, e.g. Jennes, Sherif. 5. Consistent, flexible, committed and relevant. 6. Social impact theory: strength, status, immediacy (proximity).

Obedience 1

To obey is to do as instructed, usually in response to an individual (a leader) rather than a group. Unlike conformity, obedience is less likely to involve any change in private beliefs. The advantages of obedience to the individual include less aggravation and more acceptance from others. However, disadvantages include less control of your own behaviour and doing things you don't want to. Advantages for society include greater social order, whilst disadvantages include lack of dissent and therefore no pressure for social change.

Studies into obedience to authority

Stanley Milgram 1963

Attempted to explain the horrors of the Second World War (1939–1945) when the Nazis slaughtered six million Jews, Slavs, gypsies and homosexuals. His study is probably the most controversial research in psychology. The Core Study on page 54 outlines the factors influencing the willingness for blind obedience in his study.

The original study represents a baseline situation, with 20 subsequent experiments systematically varying different aspects to illuminate the findings of the original.

Experiment	Variation	Obedience (%)
Initial	Baseline: remote victim	65.0
2	Vocal feedback only	62.5
3	2 teachers (participant reads words, confederate administers shocks)	92.5
4	Run-down setting (not prestigious university)	47.5
5	Proximity (same room as victim)	40.0
6	Absent experimenter (telephoned orders)	20.0 (lots of cheating)
7	Social support (2 other teachers/confederates who refused to obey)	10.0

Hofling et al. 1966

Provides evidence in support of Milgram's findings in a more ecologically valid setting.

- Nurses were asked (by 'Dr Smith', via telephone) to give potentially lethal injections to patients.
- Despite the regulations stating that Nurses should only take instructions from doctors they knew and the fact that the dosage was clearly stated on the bottle, 21 out of 22 appeared prepared to do it!

Bickman 1974

- Pedestrians in New York were asked by male experimenters to comply with requests such as 'pick up the bag for me'.
- Experimenters were dressed as (a) a guard, (b) a milkman or (c) in a sports coat.
- More people complied with the request from the guard than from the other two.
- Supporting Milgram's findings that perceived authority is an important factor when considering obedience levels.

Cross-cultural research: Meeus and Raaijmakers 1995

- Measured obedience in Holland.
- Participants were asked to role-play being an interviewer under the pretence that they were helping to measure the coping strategies of job applicants.
- They were asked to make statements such as 'the job is too stressful for you', in order to cause distress to the applicants.
- The interviewee (confederate) became increasingly distressed by the comments, but 22/24 participants continued to make all 15 stressful remarks.

Explanations for obedience

Dispositional factors: within the individual

Authoritarian personality: Adorno et al. 1950

- Rigid beliefs in conventional values.
- Submissive attitudes towards authority figures.
- General hostility towards other groups.
- Intolerance of ambiguity.
- More likely to be prejudiced and more likely to obey an authority figure.

The F Scale – Adorno

- The Fascism Scale is a questionnaire devised to measure attitudes of authoritarian personality. E.g. Do you agree with the statement 'sex crimes against children should be punished more harshly than mere imprisonment'?
- 2000 participants: high scores on F Scale corresponded to high scores on scale measuring prejudice and high levels of shocks given.

Early experiences

- The authoritarian personality develops through early childhood: over-hostility from parents causes the child to unconsciously internalise this hostility.
- Freud calls this repressed anger, which can then be displaced on to non-hostile minority groups (prejudice).

Personality traits that may account for resistance to obedience:

- Crowne and Marlowe 1964: low need for social approval – high self-esteem with a high opinion of self and one's own judgements.

We tend to make the **fundamental attribution error** – attributing causes of behaviour to dispositions (e.g. personality) and ignoring situational factors, which could actually have a much stronger role to play.

Individual differences.

- Not everybody obeys blindly and many individual differences have been found (35% of Milgram's participants stopped before 450V of shock).

Situational explanations: within the environment

Milgram, amongst others (e.g. Zimbardo) proposes situational factors as being most important.

- **Graduated commitment**: gradually moving from fairly simple requests that appear quite reasonable (15V shocks) to more unreasonable requests (450V).
- A **socially obedient environment**: past experience has taught us that authority figures are generally legitimate and trustworthy.
- The **agentic state**: acting as an agent for someone else, thereby not according to one's own conscience. This takes away any responsibility – 'I was only following orders'. The autonomous state is the opposite and refers to being aware of the consequences of our own actions.

Remaining in an autonomous state is easier when other people around you are behaving autonomously. When one person resists obedience it is easier for others to do so too. Milgram found that when confederates were asked to refuse, the level of obedience for the participants dropped from 65% to only 10%.

Gameson et al. 1982 – asked participants to discuss moral issues concerning a PR firm and the lifestyle of a manager of an oil company. They were videotaped and soon realised they were being manipulated so that only positive remarks were recorded. All participants rebelled; possibly because:

a) one spontaneous rebel influenced others;
b) groups of people resist easier than individuals;
c) historical time when Americans were more aware of unjust authority;
d) person in charge had little 'authority'.

EXAMINER'S TOP TIP

Sum up the evidence for high levels of obedience and its explanations.

Quick test

1. *What are the advantages and disadvantages to society of high obedience levels?*
2. *What evidence is there that the prestigious setting of Yale University increased obedience levels?*
3. *What is meant by 'dispositional explanations'?*
4. *What is meant by the 'fundamental attribution error'?*
5. *What is an 'agentic' state?*
6. *What circumstances help people remain in an autonomous state?*

1. Advantages – greater social order. Disadvantages – lack of dissent so no pressure for social change. 2. Milgram's experiment 4: run-down setting = 47.5% obedience compared to 65% at Yale. 3. Explanations focusing on the individual, e.g. personality. 4. Attributing causes of behaviour to dispositions and ignoring situational factors. 5. Acting as an agent for someone else, thereby not acting according to own conscience. 6. When others around you are acting independently and resisting obeying.

Obedience 2

This spread covers the original study into obedience by Stanley Milgram 1963.

Stanley Milgram 1963

Aim

To discover why people obey authority.

Method

Participants

- Self-selected – newspaper advert – 500 New Haven (USA) men.
- Final group: 40 men, variety of backgrounds. Believed they were taking part in a study of memory and learning at Yale University. They were paid $4.50.

Design

- Baseline experiment or a controlled observational study.
- Tape recorders, photographs and video – additional observers via one-way mirrors.
- Interviewed after experiment.
- Experimental situation was same for all participants.

I/V: experimenter's prods.
D/V: degree of obedience.

Procedure

- Confederates as 'experimenter' and 'victim/learner'.
- Fixed selection; participant always drew the slip marked 'teacher'.
- Separate rooms: learner strapped to shock chair; teacher in front of shock generator.
- Learner responded to questions (paired words):
  - correct response = move on to the next word on the list;
  - incorrect response = tell learner correct answer and then level of punishment they were going to give them.
- Teacher would then press the first lever on the shock generator.
- Teacher moved one lever up the scale of shocks for every subsequent incorrect answer.

Teacher was able to hear the learner protesting and shouting out his discomfort. Unknown to the teacher, no shocks were actually given – the cries of the learner were taped.

Experimenter gave prods if participants asked for advice:

- Prod 1: 'Please continue' or 'Please go on'.
- Prod 2: 'The experiment requires that you continue'.
- Prod 3: 'It is absolutely essential that you continue'.
- Prod 4: 'You have no other choice, you must go on'.

Results

Over half of the participants (26/40 or 65%) went all the way with the electric shocks. Only nine of the participants (22.5%) stopped at 315 volts.

- Many of the participants showed signs of nervousness and tension.
- A number had laughing fits.
- Three participants had uncontrollable seizures.

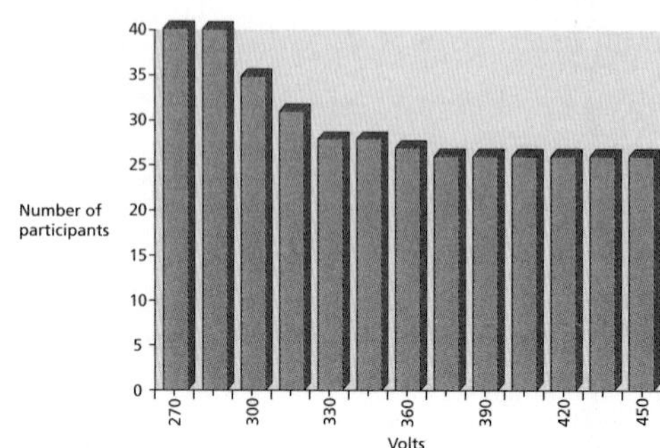

Conclusions

Features of the study that contributed to the obedience rate:

- location of the study,
- purpose of the experiment,
- social obligations,
- payment,
- the unusual nature of the task they were performing,
- the tendency for people to accept the commands of people in authority.

Strengths

- Mixed quantitative measures with qualitative methods.
- Control plus observation of natural behaviour.

Weaknesses

- Ecological validity.
- Demand characteristics.

Ethical evaluation

- Use of deception concerning the true purpose of study.
- Right to withdraw not made clear.
- Psychological distress caused to participants – not screened beforehand to see likely effects of stress.
- But – psychometric tests to confirm that participants were unharmed. Fully debriefed and reconciled with other protagonists.
- Follow-up study – no-one showed signs of long-term harm.
- Endorsement of the study by the American Psychological Association.
- Has contributed to our understanding – 'the ends justify the means'.

Applications

- Raises fundamental issues about human behaviour, such as accepting responsibility for our actions.
- The power of social situations to make us act in uncharacteristic ways.

Experimental and ecological validity

Issues associated with social research

Holland and Barratt wrote a paper on the ecological validity of laboratory deceptions. They used the term ecological validity to cover **experimental** and **mundane realism**.

Experimental realism

If an experiment forces participants to take the situation seriously and involves them in the procedures, it has achieved experimental realism.

Demand characteristics: responding to the cues in the experiment itself.

- Orne and Holland claim that participants do not take any experimental situation at face value.
- In Milgram's study, participants do not really believe that the learner is receiving painful shocks; they were responding to the demands of the social psychology experiment. However, Milgram suggests that the participants were clearly experiencing real distress at the situation and therefore were taking the situation seriously.

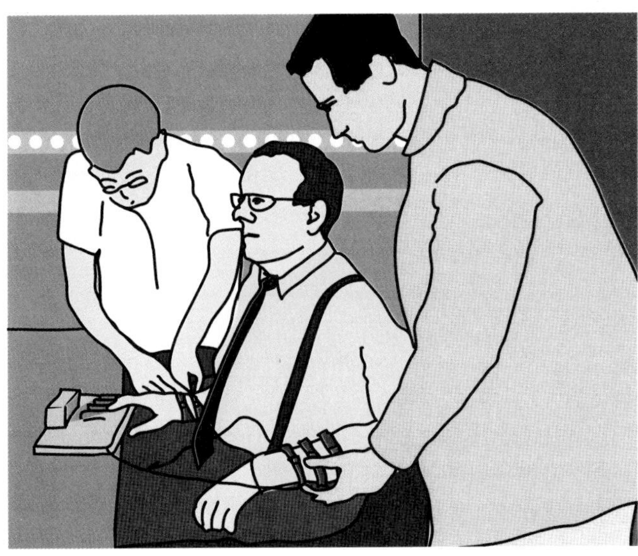

Mundane realism

The similarity of the laboratory experiment to the events that commonly happen to people in the real world.

- Orne and Holland argue that the experimental situation is unique as a context for eliciting behaviour and so we cannot generalise from it.
- Obedience shown reflects implicit trust in the experimenter and does not tell us how participants will behave outside the experimental situation.

However, experiments are then the same as any other situations composed of subordinate roles – people respond on the basis of their relationship to the person giving the orders. In this sense the demands of an authority figure are the same whether the setting is artificial or occurring naturally.

- Bickman's field study into obedience and Hofling's field experiment could arguably have more ecological validity as they were carried out in more natural surroundings.
- However, the findings were not replicated in other situations, whereas Milgram's were. As this is the criterion set for a study to be ecologically valid, one could argue that Milgram's study was more valid than the others!

EXAMINER'S TOP TIP

Try to apply the issues of realism to other studies within the course.

Quick test

1. *Identify two reasons suggested by Milgram for the high obedience rate in his study.*
2. *What is meant by the term 'experimental realism'?*
3. *Why was Bickman's study more ecologically valid than Milgram's?*
4. *In Milgram's original study, what did the participants think they were testing?*
5. *What percentage of Milgram's participants continued to the highest level?*
6. *How did Milgram justify the unethical nature of his study?*

1. Any two of place, purpose, obligation, payment, deceit, role of parties, lack of precedent. 2. If an experiment forces participants to take the situation seriously. 3. It was carried out in a real-life setting (street) therefore more mundane realism. 4. The role of punishment in learning. 5. 65% went all the way to 450V. 6. The ends justify the means.

Social cognition

The system of mental constructs and strategies that are shared by group members – those collective mental operations involved in the representation and understanding of social objects.

Memory and impression formation

- Social schema (or existing categories in our memory) direct how new information about people is perceived, interpreted and remembered later on.
- **Social comparison theory** suggests that we learn a lot about ourselves by comparison with others.
- Our perception of ourselves is learned from labels about the self from 'reflected appraisals' or the feedback we receive from others, sometimes called 'the looking-glass self' – contributes to self-esteem.

Asch's (1946) configural model

Impressions using some kind of gestalt or 'whole picture', with each piece of information influencing the others, e.g.

an intelligent and warm person generates a positive impression;

an intelligent and cold person generates a negative impression.

The cold and warm traits (central traits) have a strong influence on the interpretation of the surrounding traits.

- **Primacy effect**: traits that appear first can have more impact (first impressions).
- **Recency effect**: what appears last can also have a major impact on how we remember people.

Stereotypes

- A rigid prototype applied to large social groups, which ranks the group in a social hierarchy or stratification system.
- Cognitive consistency is culturally specific, i.e. it refers to what members of a culture or subculture consider to be logically related, not what is actually the case.

Attribution theory

Kelley's covariation model (1967)

To determine the cause of a person's behaviour, observers need three kinds of information – CCD:

- **Consensus**: How many other people behave in the same way?
- **Consistency**: Does the person always carry out that behaviour?
- **Distinctiveness**: Does that behaviour only occur in the presence of that stimulus?

Consensus = low, Consistency = high, Distinctiveness = low – dispositional attributions.

Consensus = high, Consistency = high, Distinctiveness = high – situational attributions.

Kelley's causal schemata model (1972)

If we don't have information about CCD we make attributions by slotting behaviour into 'causal schemata' – stereotyped explanations based on past experience. Two types:

- **Multiple sufficient causes**: any number of causes sufficient to cause behaviour – discounting principle used to eliminate unlikely causes.
- **Multiple necessary causes**: many causes necessary to produce a behaviour.

Correspondent inference theory

Three factors influence people to make a dispositional attribution (a correspondent inference) for behaviour rather than a situational attribution: the behaviour must be unexpected, freely chosen and have many consequences.

Attributional biases

- The **fundamental attribution error**: tendency for perceivers to underestimate the impact that situations have on people's behaviours and, instead, to attribute behaviours to personal causes.
- The **actor/observer effect**: tendency for observers to make dispositional attributions for an actor's behaviour and for actors to make situational attributions for their own behaviours.
- **Self-serving bias**: tendency to take credit (dispositional) when things go right and deny responsibility (situational) when things go wrong.

Social roles (Haney, Banks and Zimbardo)

A study in a simulated prison – Haney, Banks and Zimbardo 1973

Aim

To establish whether our behaviour is due to disposition (personality) or to the situation we find ourselves in.

Method

- Simulated prison in the University basement.
- Detailed observation through one-way mirror, video, audio tapes.

Participants

- Self-selected: 24 student volunteers (newspaper ad) paid $15/day.
- Screened to eliminate psychological problems, medical disabilities or history of crime/drugs.

Procedure

- Randomly assigned roles of either 'prisoner' or 'guard' and given appropriate uniforms.
- Rules memorised: work assignments, line up for 'count' on each new guard shift.

Results

- The prison was 'internalised': participants started to believe in it.
- Participants adopted behaviour appropriate to their roles.

Effects on the guards: pathology of power

- Enjoyment of power – became more and more tyrannical.
- Not all guards initiated aggressive acts, but none contradicted their use.

Explanation

- The illusion of 'power' had become real and legitimised by the role.
- The most hostile guards became leaders and role models.

Effects on the prisoners: pathological prisoner syndrome

- All showed negative emotions and passive and dependent behaviours.
- Half showed signs of depression, crying, fits of rage, and acute anxiety (five needed to be released early).

Zimbardo's explanation

- 'Deindividuation' – loss of personal identity.
- Unpredictable – prisoners showed signs of 'learned helplessness'.
- Dependency and emasculation – permission required for all activities, which took away their masculinity (weakened them).

Ended after 6 days rather than projected 14. An outsider pointed out ethical objections to Zimbardo, who had also internalised his role of 'prison warden'.

Zimbardo's conclusions

- Conditions in prisons are not caused by the personalities of the people in them but by the situation – situational attribution.
- Major implications for 'responsibility'.
- Visit www.Zimbardo.com

Strengths and weaknesses

- Ecological validity – differences between the simulation and real prison life (mundane realism).
- Experimental realism good – most participants felt that the experiment was real (including Zimbardo!): In private conversations, 90% was about the prison. Prisoners also referred to themselves by number.

Quick test

1. *What are 'reflected appraisals' and what effect do they have?*
2. *What attributions will lead to us making a dispositional attribution?*
3. *How were Zimbardo's participants divided into 'guards' and 'prisoners'?*
4. *What is meant by the term 'pathology of power'?*
5. *What explanation is given for the pathological prisoner syndrome?*

1. Feedback we receive from others helps form perceptions of self and contributes to self-esteem. 2. Consensus = low, consistency = high, distinctiveness = low (Kelley's covariation model) or the behaviour must be unexpected, freely chosen and have many consequences (correspondent inference theory). 3. Randomly. 4. Enjoyment of perceived legitimate power over others. 5. Deindividuation, unpredictable use of power, dependency and emasculation.

Attitudes and prejudice

An attitude may be defined as 'a psychological tendency that is expressed by evaluating a particular entity with some degree of favour or disfavour' (Eagly and Chaiken 1993).

Structure and function of attitudes

- **Cognitive**: an attitude might be formed through direct or indirect experience that provides us with information.
- **Affective**: an attitude might be formed by feelings or lead us to develop feelings about it.
- **Behavioural**: self-perception theory (Bem 1972) – we infer attitudes based on observation of our own behaviour.

Functional approach

Katz (1960): attitudes can be understood in terms of the functions that they serve, e.g. a need to express ourselves, to organise knowledge or to enhance our self-image.

Measuring attitudes

- Attitudes are not directly observable: they can only be inferred,
- Measures can be 'direct': attitude scales such as Likert scales or the semantic differential.
- Measures can be 'indirect': physiological measures such as galvanic skin response and facial electromyography.

Attitudes and behaviour

LaPiere 1934: demonstrated that behaviour does not always follow from attitudes.

Attitude change

- **Cognitive dissonance** (Festinger 1957): perceived inconsistency in cognitions causes dissonance, an uncomfortable feeling that motivates people to re-establish cognitive consistency.
- **Persuasion**: attitudes can change through persuasive communication – can be influenced by **source** (credibility, attractiveness and similarity), by **content** (arguments, appealing to emotions) and by **audience factors** (intelligence, gender, age, culture – e.g. Janis and Hovland 1959).

Prejudice and discrimination

- Prejudice is an **attitude** held prior to direct experience.
- It leads to **discrimination** (prejudiced behaviour).

Four major theories of prejudice

- Cognitive approach (inevitable given the way our minds work – stereotyping is fast).
- Individual approach, e.g. the authoritarian personality.
- Psychodynamic approach (projecting own feelings onto 'scapegoat').
- Intergroup approach (favour own group to increase own self-esteem).

Ethnocentrism

- The tendency to feel hostility towards out-group members and to undervalue their products.
- The tendency for increased liking for in-group members plus pressure for conformity and group cohesion and to overvalue the products of the in-group (any group we belong to).

Two types of intergroup conflict

Rational

- A means to an end: genuine competition between groups with divergent interests (e.g. scarce social resources – competition for housing, jobs).
- 'Realistic' group conflict theory: Sherif's famous 'Robber's cave' study (1961) – boys split into two groups engaging in competitive activities with conflicting goals (football, tug-of-war, etc.). Intergroup hostility emerged very quickly and almost automatically.

Irrational

- An end in itself; serves to release accumulated emotional tensions of various kinds (scapegoat).
- **Social identity theory** assumes that group members have a basic need for a positive social identity and that intergroup conflicts arise because each group inevitably compares itself to the other – Tajfel 1981 (see Core Study opposite).

EXAMINER'S TOP TIP

You need to be able to tell the difference between prejudice and discrimination.

Intergroup discrimination – Tajfel 1970

Aim

To provide support to 'minimal group theory' – merely being categorised can create intergroup rivalry. Discriminatory behaviour can occur even if no prejudice is present.

Method

Laboratory experiments.

I/V: the group of the participant – overestimator/underestimator of dots or preferring Klee/Kandinsky.

D/V: the points awards.

Participants

First experiment 64 schoolboys from Bristol, age range 14–15 years; second experiment 48 boys – all knew each other well.

Procedure

Experiment 1

- Groups of eight estimated numbers of dots.
- Randomly assigned to either an overestimating or an underestimating group.

Experiment 2

- Groups of 16 rated paintings.
- Randomly assigned to a group preferring Klee or Kandinsky.

Both experiments

Participants had to award points to pairs of boys. They were given booklets containing matrices (e.g. see below). They had to choose one column of points to be awarded (e.g. 2 points to no. 1, 4 points to no. 6). At the end, each boy received his total points in real money.

Boy no. 1	4	2	0	1	4	9
Boy no. 6	9	4	1	0	2	4

There were three possible choices:

- **in-group** – both boys from his own group;
- **out-group** – both boys from the other group;
- **intergroup** – one boy from each group.

Results

Experiment 1

- In-group or out-group choices: maximum fairness shown (e.g. 0 and 1 in the matrix above).
- Intergroup choices: most boys gave their own group most.

Experiment 2

- Different set of matrices used (see below) to assess which of three variables had the greatest effect.
- Maximum in-group profit (MIP) – largest award to members of the in-group (e.g. 16 and 7).
- Maximum joint profit (MJP) – largest award to both boys (e.g. 12 and 15).
- Maximum difference (MD) – largest difference in favour of the in-group (e.g. 16 and 7).

Boy no. 8 (in-group)	16	15	14	13	12
Boy no. 3 (out-group)	7	9	11	13	15

- Most boys chose MD, then MIP; very few chose MJP.
- Boys left with **less** money than if they had awarded on basis of best for all (MJP)!

Conclusion

- Out-group discrimination is very easy to trigger – mere categorisation is enough!

Strengths and weaknesses

- Biased sample – all boys, same age, from same school.
- Ecological validity – artificial setting – not like real life.
- Demand characteristics – why state which group the boys belong to?

Ethics

- No informed consent; deception.
- Right to withdraw.

EXAMINER'S TOP TIP
Be prepared to identify MIP, MJP and MD on any new matrix.

Quick test

1. ***What are the functions of attitudes?***
2. ***How do we measure attitudes?***
3. ***What did Sherif suggest caused intergroup hostility?***
4. ***How did Tajfel provide evidence against Sherif's 'realistic groups' theory?***
5. ***Why did Tajfel's participants go home with less money than they could have done?***

1. So we can express ourselves, organise our knowledge or enhance our self-image. 2. Using self-reports, e.g. attitude scales like the Likert scale or the semantic differential. 3. Competition between two groups, perhaps over scarce resources. 4. He showed that mere categorisation is enough to cause intergroup discrimination. 5. They chose maximum difference in favour of own group instead of maximum joint profit.

Ethical issues within social psychology

- **Ethics – moral behaviour of professionals.**
- **Morals – everyday standards of what is right and wrong.**

Informed consent
Not always possible in social psychology as awareness of the experiment can lead to demand characteristics.

Deception
Often used in social psychology as a means of gaining ecologically valid results. Prior general consent and presumptive consent can both be used as a way of overcoming objections to deception: e.g. Gamson et al. 1982, in their study of resistance to obedience, asked volunteers before the study for general consent to be deceived.

Debriefing
Most social psychology studies involve a thorough debriefing after the study – vital if deception has been used. However, field experiments such as Piliavin's do not always debrief participants – not always practical and some would argue that 'what you don't know cannot hurt you'.

The right to withdraw
Because deception is often used, the right to withdraw is not always made clear to participants. However, after debreifing, consent can be sought and if the participant is not happy about his results being used, he should be given the right to withdraw them.

Protection of participants
Participants are not always protected from physical and psychological harm (stress). However, debriefing should aim to leave the participants in the same state as they entered the study.

EXAMINER'S TOP TIP
Apply each ethical guideline to other studies within social psychology.

Confidentiality
This is usually possible. However, many social studies involve video or audio recordings, in which confidentiality is not always possible. Permission should be sought to use any form of data that contains personal information.

Socially sensitive research
The results of social research may be used by others: for this reason the publication of results should be carefully thought through beforehand and the consequences considered.

'The ends justify the means' (Milgram 1963)
- Baumrind 1964, among others, attacked the ethics of Milgram's study.
- Milgram answered his critics by reporting the results of a follow-up survey of the participants carried out 1 year later: 84% said they were 'glad to have taken part'; 1.3% said they were very sorry to have been in the experiment.
- A psychiatrist reported no long-term effects on any participants 1 year after the study.

The cost-reward model
- Milgram did not **intend** to cause distress and was surprised at the results.
- Weigh up the costs (to the participant) and the rewards (knowledge gained). If the rewards outweigh the costs then the study can be justified.
- Although Milgram used this argument to justify his experiments others still disagree. Zimbardo's prison experiment attracted more criticism which Zimbardo pointed out was probably due more to the disturbing insights into human nature rather than the experiment itself.

Good Samaritanism

An underground phenomenon? – Piliavin, Rodin and Piliavin 1969

Aim

Background
In 1964 Kitty was fatally stabbed in New York. Although there were 38 witnesses, no-one helped! Why?

Social impact theory – Latané 1981
- **Diffusion of responsibility** occurs when many witnesses are present.
- The responsibility is 'diffused' (spread out) between people.
- Everyone thinks someone else will help – also known as the **bystander effect**.

Aim
To investigate the effect on the speed and frequency of helping, and the race or gender of the helper, of:
- type of victim (drunk or ill);
- race of victim (black or white);
- presence of model helper;
- size of the witnessing group.

Good Samaritanism continued

Method

Field experiment (103 'experimental trials') – took place on trains – journey time 8 minutes.

Participants

Passengers on New York subway.

Procedure

Teams of four student experimenters: two male actors (victim and model), two female observers.

- 70 seconds after train left station the victim pretended to collapse.
- Victim waited for help.
- If no-one helped, the model helped the victim off at the next stop.
- Observers recorded race, age, sex and location of helper passengers.

Conclusions and explanations

- The diffusion of responsibility hypothesis is **not supported**, perhaps because victim could be seen.
- Characteristics of the victim may contribute to our decision to help or not.
- If rewards for helping outweigh costs of helping we are likely to act in a pro-social manner (help).

The cost-reward model

- The emergency created a state of emotional arousal, heightened by empathy with victim, being close to situation, length of emergency.
- This arousal state will be interpreted as fear, sympathy or disgust.
- Can be reduced by moving away, helping or deciding the victim is undeserving of help.

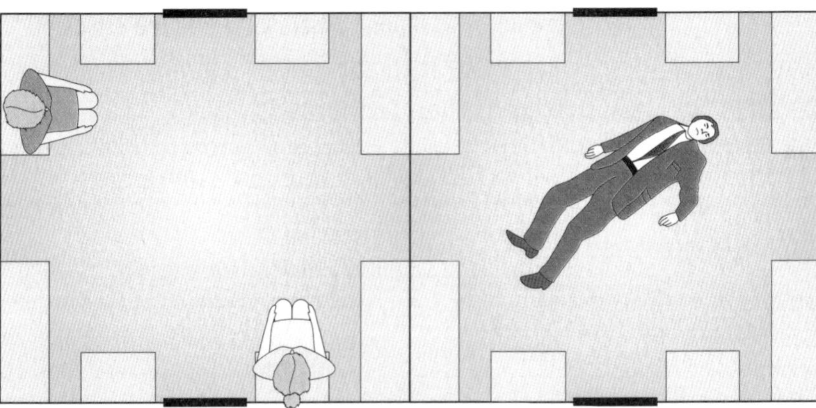

Strengths and weaknesses

- Good ecological validity – natural setting.
- Standardised procedure – Student experimenters were very reluctant to act out the 'drunk' condition.
- Lack of control over extraneous variaxbles such as individual differences in participants.

Results

- Victim received spontaneous help 93% of the time.

Type of victim/helper

- 100% help (95% spontaneous) for 'ill' victim carrying cane; 81% help (50% spontaneous) for 'drunk' victim.
- Help faster for 'ill' victim.
- More same-race helpers, particularly in 'drunk' condition.
- Males helped more than females.

Alternative method

- Laboratory experiment could control for individual differences and control the independent variables much better, but lack of ecological validity.

Ethics

- Deception of participants and lack of informed consent.
- No right to withdraw.
- No debriefing.
- Provoked anxiety and inconvenience.

Quick test

1. *Why did Piliavin et al. choose to conduct a field experiment?*
2. *Why did more males than females help in the underground study?*
3. *Why did Piliavin not find diffusion of responsibility?*
4. *What did Milgram mean when he said 'the ends justify the means'?*
5. *Why is informed consent difficult to obtain in social research?*

1. To increase ecological validity by studying behaviour in real-life situations. 2. The cost-reward model suggests the costs of helping would be less for males. 3. Perhaps because the victim could be seen. 4. The end result or findings from a study can be so worthwhile that the means by which they are obtained (perhaps unethical) can be justified. 5. Knowing the intentions of the study can lead people to behave in unnatural ways, perhaps responding to demand characteristics rather than naturally.

Practice questions

Use these to test your progress. Check your answers on pages 92–95.

Social psychology

1 Explain the difference between obedience and conformity. [2]

....

2 Evaluate the research into majority influence. [2]

....

3 Give two situational explanations for conformity. [2]

....

4 According to Kelley's attribution theory, what circumstances would lead to minority influence? [2]

....

5 Explain why Hofling's 1966 study is more ecologically valid than Milgram's study into obedience. [2]

....

6 Outline a study that confirms Milgram's findings, that perceived authority is an important factor when considering obedience levels. [2]

....

7 Outline a dispositional explanation for obedience. [4]

....

....

....

....

8 Outline the main features of Milgram's original study that led to high levels of obedience. [3]

....

....

....

9 Evaluate the ethics of Milgram's study into obedience. [3]

....

....

....

10 What is meant by the term 'mundane realism'? [2]

....

11 What evidence does Milgram provide for the fact that participants were not responding to demand characteristics? [2]

....

12 In what way can it be argued that Milgram's study is more ecologically valid than Bickman's? [2]

....

13 What is meant by 'the looking-glass effect? [2]

....

14 What is meant by the term 'primacy effect'? [2]

....

15 What is meant by the term 'stereotype'? [2]

....

16 What is meant by the term 'causal schemata'? [3]

....

....

....

17 What evidence does Zimbardo provide in support of his study having good 'experimental realism'? [2]

....

18 How can a person's attitude be changed through persuasion? [2]

....

19 What is 'rational' intergroup conflict? [2]

....

20 What is meant by the term 'ethnocentrism'? [3]

....

....

....

21 Describe the 'minimal group theory'. [2]

....

22 What was the major variable in Tajfel's study and how was it measured? [2]

....

23 What is meant by the 'cost-reward' model of helping behaviour? [2]

....

24 How can a researcher overcome the ethical objections to the use of deception? [2]

....

25 What is 'socially sensitive research'? [2]

....

Total /56

Physiology and behaviour

Physiological psychology attempts to explain experiences and behaviour with reference to biological systems (bodily systems such as the nervous system, hormones, heart rate, etc.).

Communication across the brain

- **Neurons** form nerves. They are cells that process information and communicate with thousands of other neurons.
- **Synapses** are extremely small gaps between neighbouring neurons (nerves)
- Messages are sent across synapses by **chemical neurotransmitters**.

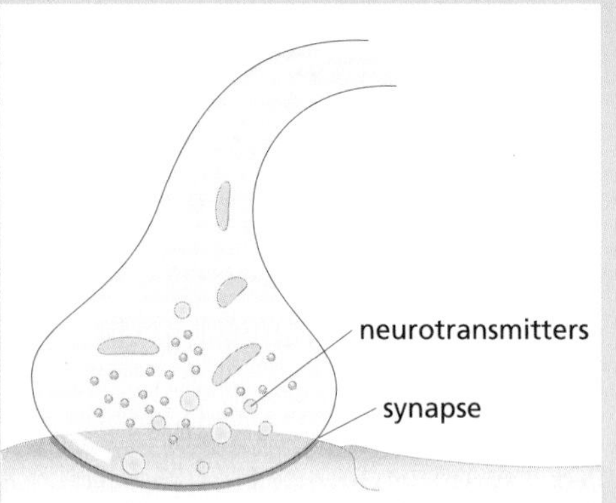

Localisation of brain function

Different areas of the brain are associated with specific functions (physical or behavioural).

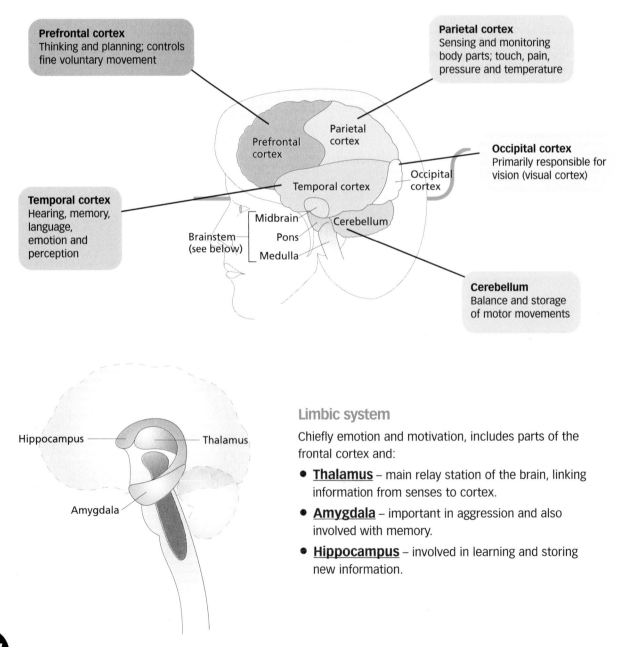

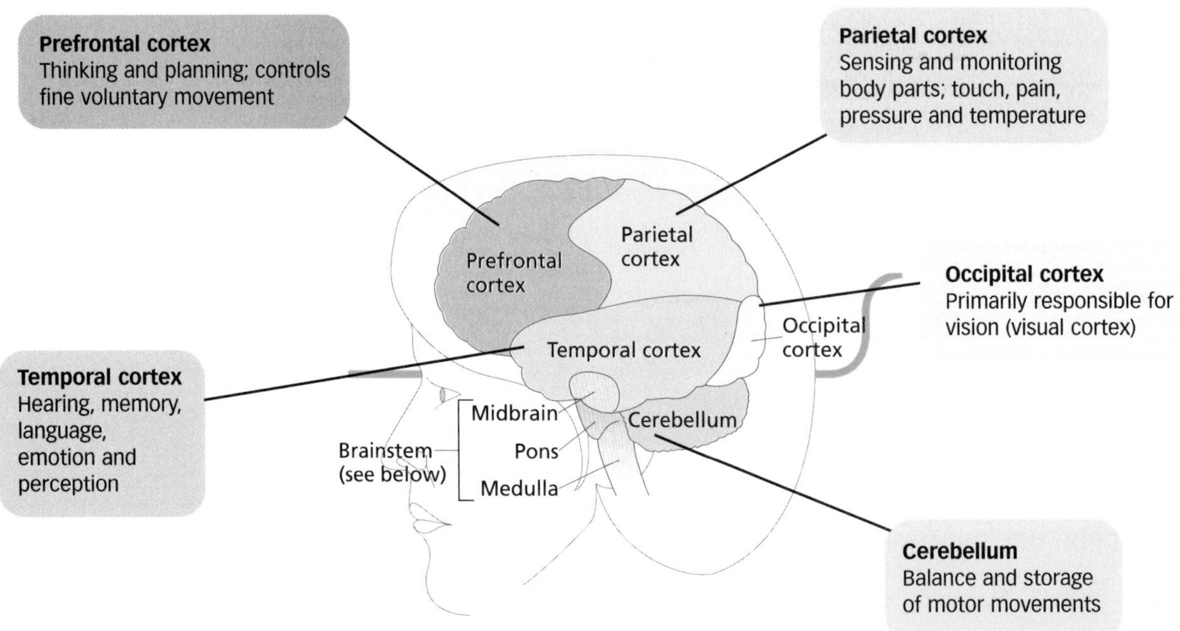

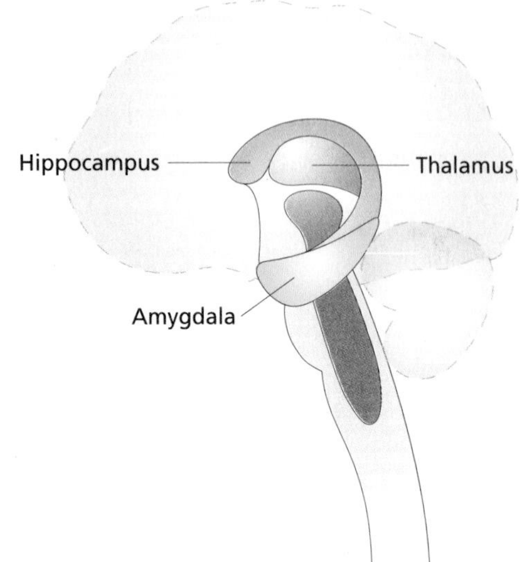

Limbic system

Chiefly emotion and motivation, includes parts of the frontal cortex and:

- **Thalamus** – main relay station of the brain, linking information from senses to cortex.
- **Amygdala** – important in aggression and also involved with memory.
- **Hippocampus** – involved in learning and storing new information.

Identifying areas of cortical specialisation

Brain imaging

MRI scans – magnetic resonance imaging.
- ✔ Quite detailed – still picture.
- ✔ Some can be used during task performance.
- ✘ Non-invasive – does not give information about activity.

PET scans – positron emission tomography.
- ✔ Detects activity levels in different places – produces coloured images.
- ✘ Invasive – require injection of mildly radioactive tracers.

Other measures

EEG – electroencephalograph.
- ✔ Non-invasive.
- ✘ Can be sensitive – only measure brain waves.

Damage
- ✔ Strokes, tumours, accidental head trauma – very ethical methods.
- ✘ Not always possible – depends on area of damage.
- ✘ Few participants.

Phineas Gage – lived after a metal pole was removed from his head. No damage, but personality altered.

Deliberate damage

Animal studies have highlighted many roles, e.g. limbic system.
- ✔ Control over specific area studied.
- ✘ Ethical issues.
- ✘ Lack of generalisability to humans.

Human studies have involved prefrontal lobotomy on mental inmates in attempts to control behaviour, and electrical stimulation.
- ✔ Control over specific area studied.
- ✘ Ethical issues.

Strengths of biological approach

Scientific approach:
- Objective – free from personal bias.
- Controlled – the use of controlled conditions.
- Replicable – being able to repeat the study in exactly the same way.
- Refutable – using aims and hypotheses that can be tested.

Can provide practical applications for effective treatment, e.g. drugs for mental disorders.

Limitations of the biological approach

Reductionism

Reduces complex behaviour to simple units.

Advantages

- Simple component parts are easy to study, test and understand.
- Reductionist explanations are often scientific and based on hard fact

Limitations

- Fails to capture the complexity of everyday experiences such as emotional responses.
- Does not explain meanings behind actions and is therefore limited.
- Humans studying humans cannot be completely bias-free.
- Scientific viewpoint can be very artificial, deterministic and ignores free will.
- Scientific methods can often be artificial.
- Natural experiments are difficult to control for extraneous variables, e.g. identical twins with identical genes often share very similar environmental conditions, so similarities are not due to genes alone.

Quick test

1. *What is meant by the term 'localisation of brain function'?*
2. *Why are PET scans often used to measure brain function?*
3. *What areas of the brain make up the limbic system?*
4. *Why are identical twins used in studies of intelligence or abnormal behaviour?*
5. *Is reductionism a strength or a weakness in psychological studies?*

1. Behavioural or physical functions are 'localised' or specific to different areas of the brain. 2. They can detect activity levels in different parts of the brain. 3. The thalamus, hippocampus and amygdala. 4. To help identify the extent to which nature (genetic inheritance) is involved. 5. Both: simple components easy to study but ignore complex interactions.

Dreams and dreaming/Emotion

This spread covers two investigations:

- **The relation of eye movements during sleep to dream activity: an objective method of the study of dreams (Dement and Kleitman 1957)**
- **Cognitive, social and physiological determinants of emotional state (Schachter and Singer 1962)**

Dement and Kleitman 1957

Aim

Three specific hypotheses:

- Significantly more dreaming occurs during **REM sleep** than during non-REM sleep.
- A significant positive correlation between the objective length of time in REM and the subjective duration of dreaming.
- A significant relationship between the pattern of eye movements and the content of the dream.

Method

Laboratory experiments including observations.

Participants: seven adult males and two adult females.

- Individuals sleep in laboratory room after normal day (but no alcohol or caffeine).
- EEG measurements of brainwaves.
- Woken and had to record their dream.
- Self-report of whether REM sleep had been for 5 or 15 minutes.
- Correlational analysis of type of eye movement and type of dream.

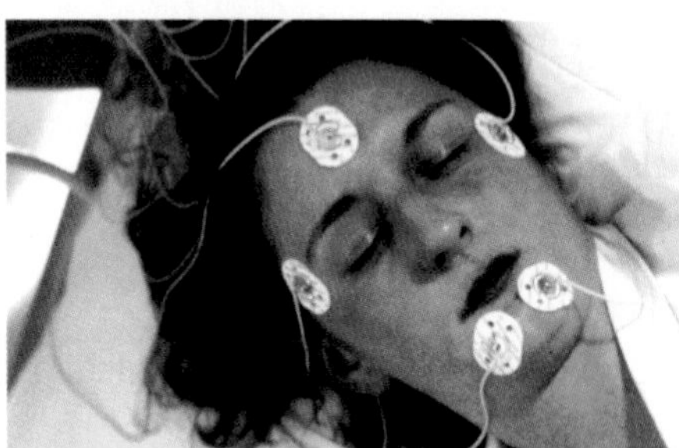

Results

1

- Woken at random, or during REM and non-REM sleep.
- More dreams reported during REM than non-REM sleep.
- Non-REM dreams were mostly within 8 minutes of a REM period.

2

- Woken 5 or 15 minutes after REM sleep.
- Participants were mostly correct at guessing the duration of their dream.

3

- Woken after different patterns of eye movements were seen.
- Strong association between pattern of REM and content of dream. E.g. vertical REM – dreams about cliff faces, ladders; horizontal REM – people playing tennis.

Conclusion

All three hypotheses were supported:

- More dreams do occur in REM rather than non-REM sleep.
- People are aware of how long they have been dreaming.
- Strong association between pattern of eye movements and content of dreams.

Strengths

- First objective study of dreams.
- Control over independent variable (REM or non-REM) in form of objective measures.
- Recorded before experimenter entered the room to avoid experimenter bias and demand characteristics.

Weaknesses

- Biased sample: very small and mostly male – lacks generalisability.
- Relies on self-reports of dreams – unreliable.
- Lack of ecological validity: artificial environment, abstaining from alcohol and caffeine.
- Lack of complete control over I/V, so difficult to identify causal relationships: e.g. dreams may occur during non-REM sleep but may be more difficult to recall because sleep is deeper.

EXAMINER'S TOP TIP

Always be prepared to give an alternative method of measuring the dependent variable.

Ethics

No issues raised.

Alternative

Case studies of individuals: write down time, duration and content of dreams in a diary. Enlist a family member to record eye movements. Improved ecological validity but less objective measurement of REM sleep.

Emotion – Schachter and Singer 1962

Aim

Three specific hypotheses highlighting **cognitive labelling theory**.

- Unexplained physiological arousal will be labelled by cognitive explanations based on the social situation.
- An appropriate explanation for physiological arousal will mean no label needed from external cues.
- Without physiological arousal no emotion will be experienced, despite social cues.

Method

Laboratory experiments.

Participants: 184 male college students (volunteered for extra points in exam).

I/V's:

- physiological arousal – epinephrine injection (adrenaline) or placebo (saline);
- explanation of arousal – informed, misinformed, or ignorant;
- social cues – euphoric or angry stooge.

D/V: experienced emotional state – measured through observations and self-reports.

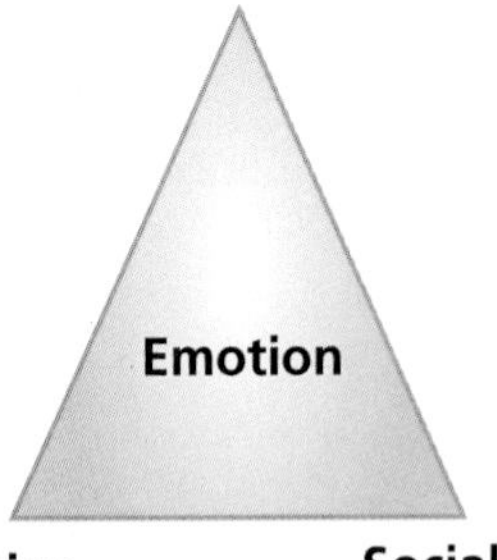

Results

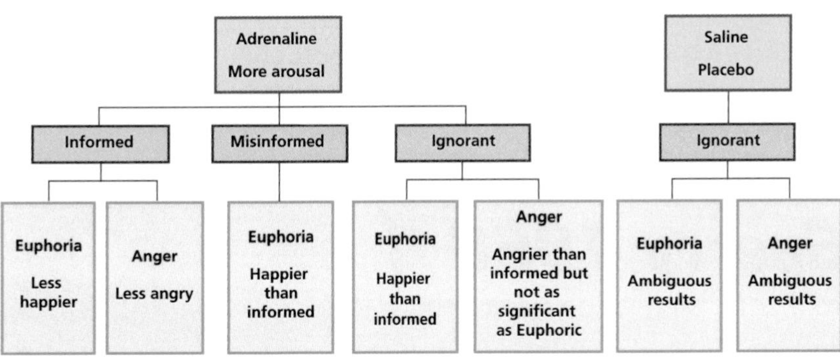

Participants informed of the true effects of adrenaline did not need to label emotional state using cognitive appraisal and social cues.

Conclusion

- People label their emotional state according to available cognitions.
- If there is no physiological arousal, cognitive cues to emotion have no effect.

Strengths

- Standardised procedure used throughout.
- Highly replicable.
- Manipulating three variables at once – identifying causal relationships.

Weaknesses

- Biased sample: male college students – lacks generalisability.
- Self-reports: lack flexibility and can be biased by motivational levels.
- Demand characteristics (particularly for angry condition – risk of not gaining extra points.
- Lack of ecological validity – unexplained physiological arousal is rare.
- Injection is artificial – may itself increase arousal.

Ethical issues

- Protection of participants: lack of medical checks before and during experiment.
- Deception: content of injection, purpose of study, stooge.
- Right to withdraw: not made clear – risk of losing extra exam points.

Alternative

- Observing bodily experiences such as clamminess of skin, stutter in voice, shaky hands, etc. – measure emotions with reduced demand characteristics.

EXAMINER'S TOP TIP

Remember the triangle. All three variables needed for emotions to occur.

Quick test

1. ***What explanation is given for dreams reported during non-REM sleep?***
2. ***How did Dement and Kleitman avoid experimenter bias and demand characteristics?***
3. ***What are the objective measures used by Dement and Kleitman?***
4. ***Why did the misinformed group in Schacter and Singer's study feel happier than the informed group?***
5. ***Why might the control group (saline only) have been physiologically aroused?***

1. They usually occurred within 8 minutes of a period of REM sleep. 2. Participants recorded content of their dream before experimenter entered room. 3. Brainwaves measured by electroencephalograph to identify REM and non-REM sleep. 4. No explanation for physiological arousal so they looked for cues in the situation. 5. The injection itself may have caused some anxiety.

Brain lateralisation and function

This spread covers two investigations:

- **Hemisphere disconnection and unity in consciousness (Sperry 1968).**
- **Brain abnormalities in murderers indicated by positron emission tomography (Raine, Buchsbaum and LaCasse 1997).**

Sperry 1968

Aim

The 'split-brain' shows characteristics during testing that suggest each hemisphere:

- has slightly different functions;
- possesses an independent stream of conscious awareness; and
- has its own set of memories inaccessible to the other.

Method

Natural experiment – independent measures design.

Participants: 11 patients who had their corpus callosum cut for medical reasons (to help epilepsy): this prevented communication between the left and right hemispheres of the brain.

I/V: corpus callosum intact/cut.

D/V: responses of participants to visual field tests – pictures presented at high speed to left or right visual field.

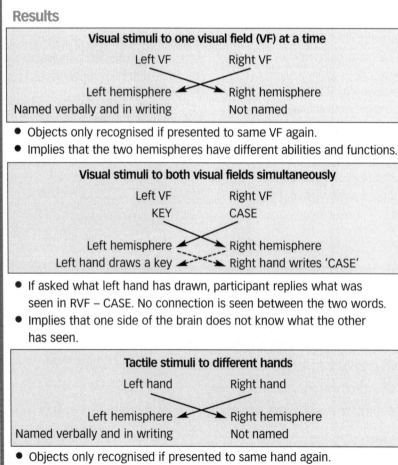

Results

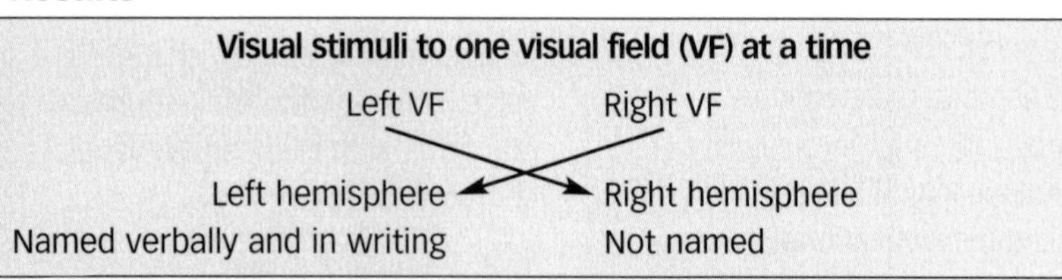

- Objects only recognised if presented to same VF again.
- Implies that the two hemispheres have different abilities and functions.

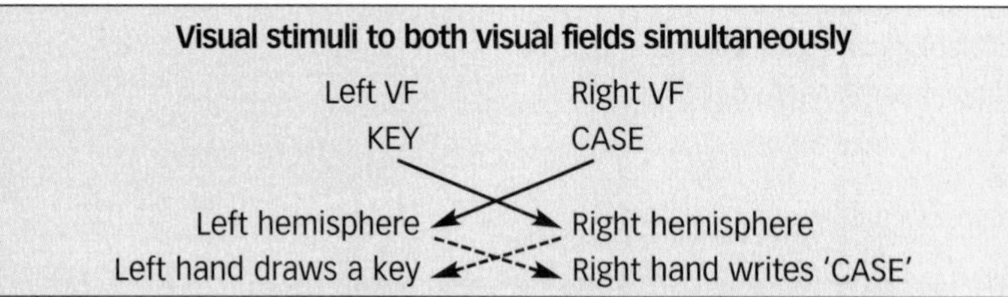

- If asked what left hand has drawn, participant replies what was seen in RVF – CASE. No connection is seen between the two words.
- Implies that one side of the brain does not know what the other has seen.

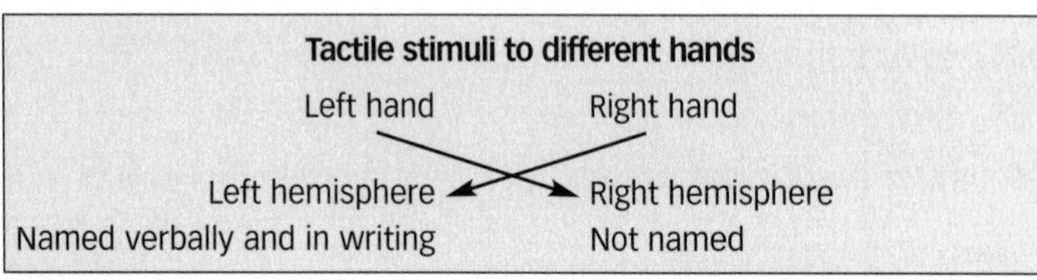

- Objects only recognised if presented to same hand again.
- Implies that one side of the brain does not know what the other has felt.

Conclusion

- Each hemisphere has different functions, e.g. left has language ability.
- Each hemisphere has its own perceptions, memories and phenomenology.
- The corpus callosum enables each hemisphere to be aware of activities in the other hemisphere.

Strengths

- Standardised procedure used throughout.
- Highly replicable.
- Controlled for extraneous variables such as visual field technique (stimulus entering one hemisphere only) – therefore able to suggest cause and effect.

Weaknesses

- Construct validity questionable: e.g. is there really lateralisation of brain function? Sperry found that the right hemisphere does have some language ability.
- Natural experiment: lack of control over variables such as individual differences.
- Some people's brains are more lateralised than others'.
- Biased sample: participants may have been atypical before the experiment – lacks generalisability.

Ethical issues

- Fairly good: patients were tested after their corpus callosum had been cut for medical reasons. Sperry **did not** deliberately cut it for experimental reasons!
- Being told of differences may have caused some distress.

Alternative

Other ways of measuring lateralised function might include the use of techniques such as PET scans, conducted whilst participants complete a task such as speaking or listening to music.

EXAMINER'S TOP TIP

Always be prepared to discuss the advantages and weaknesses of the methodology of each core study.

Raine, Buchsbaum and LaCasse 1997

Aim

To see if severely violent offenders have brain dysfunction localised to specific brain areas.

Method

Natural and laboratory experiment.

Participants: matched pairs design: 41 murderers pleading 'not guilty for reasons of insanity' (NGRI) matched for age and sex with 41 controls, including 6 schizophrenics matched with 6 schizophrenics in the murder group.

I/V: murder/non-murder.

- Injected with fluorodeoxyglucose (FDG) tracer.
- Continuous performance task started 30 seconds before the injection so that initial task novelty would not be labelled with FDG.
- After 32 minutes, transferred to PET scanner.

Results

Brain region	Glucose metabolism showed through PET	Possible effects
Prefrontal cortex	Lower glucose metabolism	Control centre: loss of self-control, impulsivity, immaturity, altered emotionality
Parietal cortex	Lower glucose metabolism in left angular gyrus	Learning deficits
Corpus callosum	Lower bilateral glucose metabolism	Inappropriate emotional expression
Amygdala	Reduced in left Greater in right	Associated with aggressive behaviour in both animals and humans (Bear 1989)
Hippocampus	Reduced in left Greater in right	Inappropriate emotional expression
Thalamus	Reduced in left Greater in right	Imbalance in relaying messages from limbic structures to prefrontal cortex

Strengths

- Sample size large for PET research.
- Well-controlled conditions and matched pairs design.
- Ruled out confounding variables of handedness, ethnicity and head injury.

Weaknesses

- Does not say anything about **causes of brain differences**.
- General problems with PET scans.
- Cannot be generalised to other types of violent offences or to other types of crime.

Ethics

Socially sensitive research: implications for treatment or future involvement in manipulating brains.

Alternative

Any other method for measuring brain function – see page 64.

Conclusion

- NGRI have significant differences in glucose metabolism in selected brain regions.
- Does **not** show that violence is **determined** by biology.

Application

Raine: possible to identify psychopaths/murderers and treat by replacing malfunctioning areas with microchip – but ethical/moral issues.

EXAMINER'S TOP TIP

Draw a picture of the brain – colour code areas with less glucose metabolism and areas with more or with no difference.

Quick test

1. *When Sperry's patients were presented with visual stimuli in the left visual field, what could they not do and why?*
2. *What is the function of the corpus callosum?*
3. *In what way might lower glucose activity in the prefrontal cortex lead to acts of aggression?*
4. *What caused the different levels of glucose activity in the NGRI's?*
5. *Why are Raine's results 'socially sensitive'?*

1. They could not name the stimulus as the information was in the right hemisphere only. 2. Communication between the left and right hemispheres of the brain. 3. Loss of self-control. 4. We don't know – the study does not tell us anything about causation. 5. Could persuade society about the possibilities of 'manipulating' brain functions in order to control behaviour – even before any criminal behaviour has taken place.

Stress

A state that occurs when people are faced with demands from their environment that they think they can't meet.

- **The hypothalamus controls the stress response and triggers a series of events in the body to prepare it to deal with the stressful situation.**
- **The sympathetic division of the autonomic system prepares us for activity by pumping adrenaline into the bloodstream.**
- **The 'fight/flight' mechanism prepares the body to respond to a threatening situation – reduces all unnecessary processes and increases energy supply to all major muscles, increases blood glucose and constricts blood vessels in the skin to limit any potential blood loss, and reduces blood flow to digestive organs.**

By measuring someone's hormone levels, psychologists can gain an insight into their levels of arousal. In general this heightened sense of arousal produced by stress will have a detrimental effect on our health by reducing the effectiveness of the immune system and increasing the risk of cardiovascular disease (heart attacks) and stomach ulcers.

Stress and physical illness

Research into the relationship

Selye's General Adaptation Syndrome 1952: GAS = ARE

Stage 1: **A**larm reaction – the 'fight/flight' initial reaction to threat.

Stage 2: **R**esistance – arousal down but still not normal – attempt to adapt and resist. Stress hormones reduce effectiveness of immune system.

Stage 3: **E**xhaustion – if situation continues, body's energy reserves finally become depleted and this lowers resistance still further.

Stress is the most significant factor in lowering resistance and triggering the various mechanisms involved in disease.

Criticisms

- Is the response the same regardless of the stressor (could be cataclysmic, personal, ambient)?
- Severity and duration of response.
- Individual coping mechanisms.

Brady's monkeys 1958

Monkeys placed in an apparatus that gave electric shocks at regular intervals. One monkey could prevent the shocks by pushing a lever (the executive monkey), whilst the other had no control at all.

- The executive monkeys died from stomach ulcers while the passive monkeys did not.
- Suggests that the high stress of having to push the lever caused the ulcers.
- Note that the ulcers burst and killed monkeys during rest period – parasympathetic system kicks in and increases digestive activity.

Quick test

1. *Which part of the brain triggers the stress response?*
2. *What is the 'fight or flight' response?*
3. *What are the 3 stages in Selye's General Adaptation Syndrome?*
4. *Why did Brady's monkeys die?*
5. *What are the long-term effects of stress?*
6. *The adrenal gland triggers which part of the nervous system?*

1. Hypothalamus. 2. Initial response to danger = raised BP, increased heart rate and respiration rate, reduced digestive activity. 3. GAS = ARE (Alarm reaction, Resistance, Exhaustion). 4. The high stress of having to push the lever to stop electric shocks caused ulcers in the executive monkeys. 5. Cardiovascular disease, stomach ulcers (Brady), less resistance to infection. 6. The sympathetic branch of the autonomic nervous system.

The physiological response to a stimulus in the environment

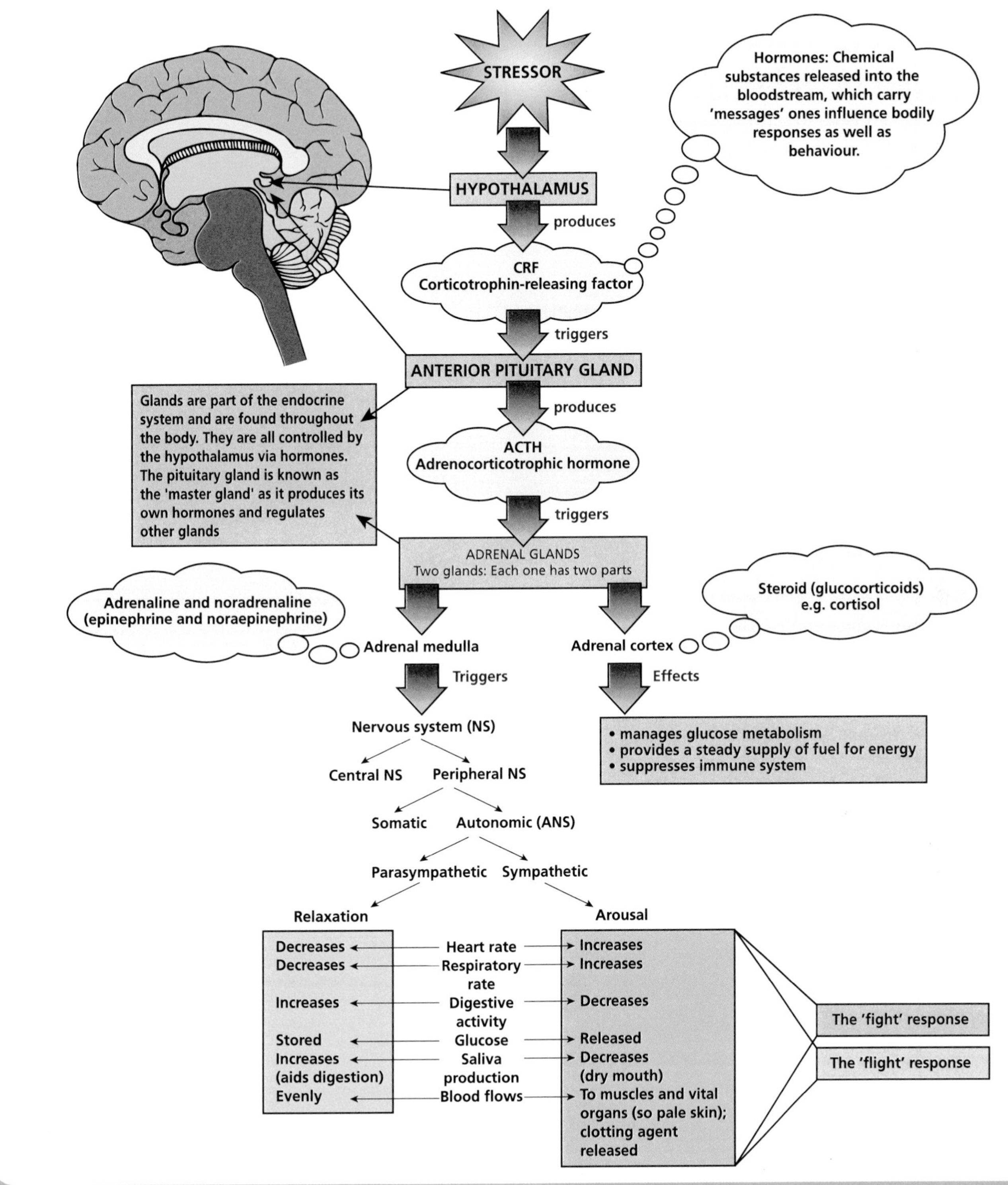
STRESSOR
Hormones: Chemical substances released into the bloodstream, which carry 'messages' ones influence bodily responses as well as behaviour.
HYPOTHALAMUS
produces
CRF
Corticotrophin-releasing factor
triggers
ANTERIOR PITUITARY GLAND
Glands are part of the endocrine system and are found throughout the body. They are all controlled by the hypothalamus via hormones. The pituitary gland is known as the 'master gland' as it produces its own hormones and regulates other glands
produces
ACTH
Adrenocorticotrophic hormone
triggers
ADRENAL GLANDS
Two glands: Each one has two parts
Adrenaline and noradrenaline (epinephrine and noraepinephrine)
Steroid (glucocorticoids) e.g. cortisol
Adrenal medulla
Adrenal cortex
Triggers
Effects
Nervous system (NS)
• manages glucose metabolism
• provides a steady supply of fuel for energy
• suppresses immune system
Central NS
Peripheral NS
Somatic
Autonomic (ANS)
Parasympathetic
Sympathetic
Relaxation
Arousal
Decreases ← Heart rate → Increases
Decreases ← Respiratory rate → Increases
Increases ← Digestive activity → Decreases
Stored ← Glucose → Released
Increases (aids digestion) ← Saliva production → Decreases (dry mouth)
Evenly ← Blood flows → To muscles and vital organs (so pale skin); clotting agent released
The 'fight' response
The 'flight' response

Quick test

1. What would make the hypothalmus produce CRF?
2. Why might prolonged stress lead to stomach ulcers?
3. Why does stress reduce the effectiveness of the immune system?
4. What effect does increased adrenaline have on the body?

1. Stressors – these can be real or perceived. 2. 'Fight or flight' response decreases digestive activity – see Brady. 3. Adrenal glands produce steroids, e.g. cortisol which suppresses immune system. 4. Arousal of the sympathetic nervous system, leading to fight/flight.

Sources of stress

A <u>stressor</u> is a stimulus in the environment that causes an individual to adapt their behaviour.

Ambient stressors

Can be defined as 'ever-present' environmental conditions such as noise levels, climate and weather conditions, urban life and overcrowded conditions. We tend to get used to **<u>ambient stressors</u>** – **<u>habituation</u>**.

Example: workplace stressors

- Studies have shown that fear of losing one's job, punitive management, interpersonal conflict and lack of control over one's role can all place pressure on an individual and lead to stress.
- Role conflict when the demands of the workplace are in direct conflict with the demands or needs of the individual.
- Role ambiguity when the different roles and responsibilities of individual staff are not made clear.
- Work overload can lead to 'burnout' – physical and emotional exhaustion accompanied by feelings of low self-worth.

Cataclysmic stressors

- Usually as a result of large-scale disasters or catastrophes.
- End result – sudden and extreme stress response by individuals affected either directly or indirectly.
- Other issues become less relevant.
- Can lead to 'Post-traumatic Stress Disorder' (PTSD).

Example: Three Mile Island

- In March 1979 an accident at the nuclear power station left people concerned about possible radioactive fallout.
- The fear remained long after the real danger had passed: local residents reported emotional distress and sleep difficulties.
- Medical reports showed higher levels of adrenaline in their urine and fewer immune cells.

Personal stressors

These range from the death of a loved one to everyday hassles and upsets like not being able to find the car keys.

Example: life changes – Holmes and Rahe

- 100 'judges' rated the life events by asking them how much change would be involved relative to marriage.
- Developed the Social Readjustment Rating Scale (SRRS) – 43 life events that seemed to precede medical illnesses.
- 400 participants rated them according to how long they thought it would take a person to readjust.
- Today it is used by asking people to indicate which event they have experienced in the past 12 months.
- A score of over 300 indicates the person is 'at risk' of a wide range of mental and physical illnesses.

Criticisms

- Correlational studies do not indicate causal relationships, i.e. we cannot be sure that the life event is **<u>causing</u>** the stress.
- Other possible variables include individual personality, coping strategies, social support.
- Data is usually collected retrospectively (after the event), so can be unreliable.

Examples from the SRRS	
Death of a spouse	100
Divorce	73
Marriage	53
Sex difficulties	39
Change in sleeping habits	16
Christmas	12

Individual differences in modifying the effects of stressors

Gender

- Most studies claim that men respond in a more negative manner towards stressors than women.
- More men than women die from coronary heart disease – possibly due to oestrogen levels.
- However, in the past, women have also tended to lead healthier lifestyles than men. As women are now catching up with men in drinking and smoking levels, we can expect to see their rate of heart disease also increase.
- Social support: a belief that we are loved will influence how we cope with stress. Women are thought to have better support networks.

Culture

- The way members of a society interact with each other seems to affect the way they respond to stressful situations.
- E.g. people live longer in Georgia (formerly part of Russia) – **Weg 1983** suggests many factors, including genetic factors and healthy lifestyle. The culture tends to also to have good social support networks.
- Black Americans are much more likely to suffer from cardiovascular disorders than black Africans and white Americans. Both biological explanations and psychosocial factors such as prejudice have been proposed to explain this.
- Blood pressure found to be higher in people living in urban areas – Cooper et al. 1999
- Resources – material and psychological – will also influence coping strategies.

Personality

Friedman and Rosenman 1959 proposed three personality types:

- Type A: competitive, ambitious – more likely to suffer heart disease.
- Type B: relaxed – less affected by stress.
- Type C: sociable but repressed. Emotion suppression is associated with stress.

Personality types assessed through structured interview measuring subjective responses and observed behaviour. At 8-year follow-up, 70% of men who had developed coronary heart disease had been categorised as type A.

EXAMINER'S TOP TIP

Revise some examples of individual differences in gender, culture and personality.

Quick test

1. ***What is role ambiguity and why is it stressful?***
2. ***What effects can a cataclysmic stressor have on an individual?***
3. ***What criticisms can be made of the Holmes and Rahe 'Life changes' questionnaire?***
4. ***Which gender is more at risk from heart disease and why?***
5. ***What personality type is more prone to suffer from stress?***

1. When the different roles and responsibilities of individual staff are not made clear – ambient stressor, so ever-present. 2. Fear, emotional distress, sleep difficulties, increased adrenaline levels and lower immunity. Long-term can lead to PTSD. 3. Correlational: no control over variables, no cause and effect identified and unreliable, retrospective data. 4. Men because of hormones, more unhealthy lifestyle, lack of social support. 5. Type A: competitive and ambitious.

Stress management

Methods of managing the negative effects of stress include physiological (drugs, biofeedback) and psychological approaches (e.g. stress-inoculation, increasing hardiness). Each method has clear strengths and weaknesses.

Selye: if individuals learn relaxation and stress management techniques, they can improve their health as well as their odds of living a disease-free life.

Physiological methods	Strengths	Weaknesses
Anti-anxiety drugs – e.g. benzodiazepines such as Valium • Alter neurotransmitters (GABA)	• Very effective in reducing stress • Easy to use • 70% of dependent users manage to give them up eventually – Ashton 1997	• Can have side effects such as drowsiness • Can lead to dependency • Can prevent dealing with the real causes • Ethical issues if given without fully informed consent
Biofeedback (Miller & DiCara 1967) • Become aware of physiological response (e.g. heart rate) – machines can be used to provide feedback • Learn to control this response (e.g. deep, slow breathing) • Apply this control in everyday situations	• Non-invasive • No side-effects • Effects of reductions in heart rate, blood pressure can be long term	• Most studies involve animals (e.g. conditioning rats) • Evidence from human studies is often confounded by the relaxation that accompanies biofeedback • Effort and commitment needed from the patient
Exercise Simple exercise routines increase the circulation; improved respiratory and heart rate	• Quick, easy, free and can be fun	• Requires commitment and motivation • Some individuals can become addicted

Psychological methods (cognitive therapies)	Strengths	Weaknesses
Stress inoculation – Meichenbaum 1977 • Cognitive/behavioural techniques used to get people to analyse and evaluate the effectiveness of their own coping strategies • Devise other more effective means of coping	• This type of self-instructional training can have long-lasting effects • Can be generalised to new situations	• Commitment • Time-consuming • Costly • Not effective with very high levels of stress
Increasing hardiness – Kobasa 1979 • Individuals taught to recognise signs of stress • Increase belief in own ability to control own life • View life changes as challenges and not threats	• Supported by empirical evidence (e.g. Sarafino 1990) • Hardiness, social support and exercise found to be most important factors	• Hardiness is difficult to assess. • Evidence focused on white, male, middle classes • Correlations – cannot identify causal relationships

The role of control

Perceived demands and perceived coping strategies

- Informational control – knowing what is going on and why.
- Decisional – making the decision for yourself.
- Behavioural – choice over how to behave.

Supported by empirical evidence, e.g. Langer and Rodin's study (1976) of elderly people in a nursing home showed how being allowed to make their own decisions improved the residents' feeling of control and decreased the likelihood of stress occurring.

Actual and perceived control

Perceived control is concerned with our 'locus of control' – Rotter 1962.

- Internal locus of control – attributing events to causes within oneself.
- External locus of control – attributing events to causes outside oneself.

Cognitive appraisal plays a major role. Perception (interpretation) is more important than the event itself.

Control is a major factor in any psychological approach to stress management.

If a person perceives themselves as having control over events they will feel less stressed.

Behaviour constraint theory – Proshansky et al. 1970

1 Perceived loss of control: a stimulus in the environment makes a person think they have lost control even though, in reality, they may not have done.

2 Reactance: psychological reactance as we try to regain control. The mere anticipation of the loss of control is enough to set off reactance.

3 Learned helplessness: if we are unsuccessful then we may slide into learned helplessness.

Learned helplessness – Seligman 1975

- Dogs learned they were helpless to escape electric shocks.
- Later, the dogs made no attempt to escape when they could.
- Past experience makes us believe we are helpless to change course of events.
- Can lead to severe depression in humans if they believe they have no control over the stressors in their environment.

EXAMINER'S TOP TIP

Discuss the extent to which control is an issue in stress management: weigh up the evidence.

Quick test

1. ***Why are drugs an unsuitable long-term solution to coping with stress?***
2. ***What is the major criticism of biofeedback techniques?***
3. ***On what are most cognitive therapies based?***
4. ***Which type of 'locus of control' is better for dealing with stress?***
5. ***What effect did making their own decisions have on the elderly residents in Langer and Rodin's study?***
6. ***What is the final outcome of continual reactance that has little perceived affect on the situation?***

1. Because of the side effects and risk of long-term dependency. 2. Evidence based on animal studies lack generalisability and human studies confounded by relaxation accompanying feedback. 3. The idea that assessing one's current coping strategies can lead to developing more effective, long-term strategies. 4. Internal. 5. Perceived control led to reduced stress levels. 6. Learned helplessness.

Practice questions

Use these to test your progress. Check your answers on pages 92–95.

Physiological psychology

1 What is the main function of the pre-frontal cortex? [2]

....

2 What is the main function of the limbic system? [2]

....

3 Outline the main methods used for measuring localised brain function. [2]

....

....

4 Outline the main features of the scientific approach to psychology. [3]

....

....

5 Evaluate the method used by Dement and Kleitman to study dreaming. [3]

....

6 Outline the major independent variables in Schacter and Singer's study into emotional state, and say how they were manipulated. [3]

....

....

....

7 Outline the conclusion drawn from Schachter and Singer's study. [2]

....

....

8 Why were demand characteristics a particular problem in Schachter and Singer's study? [2]

....

9 What was Sperry hoping to find out through his 'split-brain' experiments? [2]

....

10 Outline the major criticisms of Sperry's experiment. [2]

....

....

11 Why is Raine's study described as a natural experiment? [2]

....

12 What area of the brain is associated with aggressive behaviour? [2]

....

13 What conclusion did Raine come to about murderers' brains? [2]

....

....

14 What is meant by the term 'stress'? [2]

....

15 How does the sympathetic division of the autonomic nervous system prepare us for activity? [2]

....

....

16 What effect does raised arousal levels have on an individual? [2]

....

17 What criticisms can be made of Selye's 'General Adaptation Syndrome'? [2]

....

18 What effect does 'adrenocorticotrophic hormone' (ACTH) have on the body? [2]

....

19 What are the three main types of stressors? [3]

....

....

....

20 What are the main sources of stress in the workplace? [3]

....

....

....

21 Outline a method for measuring the degree of personal stressors for a particular individual. [3]

....

....

....

22 Outline research into individual differences in modifying the effects of stress. [4]

....

....

....

....

23 To what extent is the role of 'control' an important issue in stress management? [4]

....

....

....

Total /56

Gender

This section considers individual differences between genders, cultural groups, intelligence and self-identity as well as differences in behaviour that are considered abnormal in the light of psychological theories and the evidence provided to support them.

The psychology of gender

There are several concepts related to the psychology of gender.

- **Sex**: biologically based differences.
- **Gender**: all the meanings we assign to sex – the characteristics of sex that are socially influenced.
- **Androgyny**: Sandra Bem – exhibiting high levels of both masculine and feminine personality characteristics or undifferentiated, with few masculine or feminine characteristics – can result in greater behavioural adaptability.
- **Sex-role stereotype**: an 'overgeneralisation' of what behaviour is culturally acceptable for a gender:
  - masculine = instrumental traits (reflecting competence, rationality and assertiveness);

  - feminine = expressive traits (emphasising warmth, care and sensitivity).

- **Role and identity**: gender identity is the self-awareness that one is male or female.
- **Cultural diversity**: most societies promote instrumental traits in males and expressive traits in females – but great diversity exists.
- **Cultural relativism** (e.g. Mead 1935): gender roles depend upon the society, e.g. members of a New Guinea tribe (Tchambuli) showed the reverse of Western stereotypical gender roles.

Methods used in studying gender

Case studies
- In-depth studies of twins, families and adopted children.
- Identical twins have identical genetic make-up – if raised apart they can contribute to our understanding of behaviours that are inherited and those that are learned.
- Often lack generalisability as small biased samples used.

Cross-cultural
- Can identify 'cultural universals' (such as gender traits) and diversity across cultures (such as learned cultural behaviours).
- Help to understand the extent to which gender roles are due to nature or nurture.

Observations
- For example, parent–child interactions: **Fagot 1978** found that boys were encouraged to be independent and active, and girls to be dependent and passive.
- No direct contact.
- Open to subjective interpretation – two observers increases reliability.

Experiments
- Can control for extraneous variables such as other environmental influences.
- Causal relationships can be discovered.
- Natural experiments – can be difficult to isolate gender as the only difference between groups.

Survey/questionnaire/inventory
- Subjective experiences of gender-related issues and common patterns sought, e.g. Kohlberg's ideas of cognitive development backed up by interviewing children at various ages.
- Open to socially acceptable answers or even lying from the participants.

Content analysis
- Studying the content of previously published material.
- Useful for identifying patterns of sex-stereotyping behaviour and the causes of these socially/culturally constructed ideas.

Gender bias in theory and research

- **Androcentric** (male-biased views) are used as the 'norm' – behaviour that does not fit this norm is often not investigated.
- Researchers, sample of participants and the interpretation and publication of the results are all male-dominated areas causing gender bias:
  - alpha bias: exaggerating differences – reinforcing gender stereotypes;
  - beta bias: minimising differences – ignoring many parts of women's experiences.
- **Ethical issues**: informed/parental consent; prevention of psychological harm; confidentiality; socially sensitive research – the impact of research findings on the lives of men and women.

Explaining gender

Biological explanation

Sex chromosome patterns

Typical pattern of XX (female) and XY (male); atypical – occasionally patterns do not fit the typical pattern, e.g.:

- adrenogenital syndrome – chromosomal females who have been over-exposed to male hormones develop a male-like external appearance (e.g. **Money 1972**);
- testicular feminising syndrome – chromosomal males who are insensitive to testosterone develop a female external appearance.

Influence of androgens (e.g. testosterone) and oestrogen

Activate a particular response that differs between the sexes:

- men: increased testosterone – increased sexual excitement, aggression and spatial ability;
- women: increased oestrogen – increased sexual interest and memory; decreased oestrogen – depressed mood (e.g. pre-menstrual tension).

However, there are many limitations of the biological approach as it is difficult to remove social influence and find causal relationships.

Social learning theories

Gender role behaviour is learnt through observation of male and female social models such as parents, peers, media characters, etc. but the performance of the appropriate behaviour depends upon reinforcement.

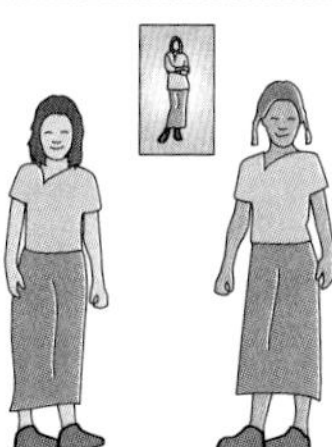

- **Modelling and imitation**: the different role-models we see around us will play a large part in the development of gender-related behaviours, e.g. Bandura.
- **Identification**: we identify with the same-sex parent and therefore we are more likely to imitate the same-sex model.
- **Reinforcement**: many gender-related behaviours are rewarded by parents, teachers and peers. Behaviours considered to be inappropriate are ignored or even punished, and therefore are not reinforced.

Cognitive developmental models

- **Kohlberg (1966)**: a child's understanding of its gender develops over time.
- Children begin to classify themselves around the age of 3 years, causing imitation of appropriate masculine or feminine behaviour.
- At about age 7 children realise that their gender remains stable over time and constant across situations – understanding of gender is complete.
- **Bem** proposes the idea of gender 'schemas'. Through interaction with the social environment young children develop ideas about the roles of each gender and these become part of cognitive 'memory'.

EXAMINER'S TOP TIP

Gender differences can be due to biology, social learning or cognitive development: try to explain the difference.

Quick test

1. *What is the difference between the terms 'sex' and 'gender'?*
2. *What is meant by the term 'androgyny'?*
3. *What is the effect of increased testosterone in males?*
4. *What is likely to make a child copy a role-model they have seen?*
5. *According to Kolhberg's cognitive development model, at what age are children aware of gender being stable and constant over time?*

1. Sex is a biological difference whilst gender is the meaning we assign to the sex of a person. 2. An individual exhibiting high levels of masculine and feminine personality characteristics, or undifferentiated (exhibiting few masculine or feminine characteristics). 3. Increased sexual excitement, aggression and spatial ability. 4. Reinforcement (reward). 5. Age 7 years.

Racial preference/intelligence

This spread covers two investigations:

- **Black is beautiful: a re-examination of racial preference and identification (Hraba and Grant 1970).**
- **A nation of morons: mis-measuring intelligence (Gould 1982).**

EXAMINER'S TOP TIP
Try to sum up results verbally and then write them down from memory.

Hraba and Grant 1970

Aim

To replicate a previous study, conducted by the Clarks in 1939, which showed that black children preferred white dolls and rejected black dolls – implying that they thought black was not beautiful and that they preferred to be white.

Method

Natural experiment.

Participants: 160 children (89 black and 71 white) aged 4–8 years, from five state schools in Lincoln, Nebraska.

I/V:

- Race (black = light, medium and dark; others = white).
- Time (as results compared to Clarks' original study).

The race of the interviewer was controlled.

D/V:

- Racial preference (questions 1–4).
- Racial identification (questions 5–7).
- Racial self-identification (question 8).

Materials: four dolls, two black and two white – otherwise identical.

Conclusions

- Black children are not necessarily white orientated.
- Negroes are becoming Blacks and prouder of their race in 1969 compared with 1939.

Strengths

- Replication of previous study – good concurrent validity.
- Standardised procedure – replicable.

Weaknesses

Can't be sure if there is change: children from Lincoln might have chosen black dolls in the original study.

- May lack validity: forced choice ignores intensity of preference – may not measure race and self-liking.
- Not generalisable: specific to one area of USA – also a 'black movement' campaign had been active in Lincoln and black children may have modelled those attitudes (Bandura and social learning theory).

Ethics

Forced choice may imply that one race is preferable to another.

Alternative

Observations of children's preferences in play activities and choices of friendships. Eliminates the possibility of socially acceptable answers from self-reports, but could show bias from observers.

Results

	Clarks (black children)	Hraba and Grant (black children)	Hraba and Grant (white children)
Racial preference: Give me the doll that… 1. you want to play with	67% white doll 32% black doll	30% white doll	(83% white doll) chose white
2. is a nice doll	59% white doll 38% black doll	46% white doll	(70% white doll)
3. looks bad	17% white doll 59% black doll	61% white doll	(34% white doll)
4. is a nice colour	60% white doll 38% black doll	31% white doll	(48% white doll)
Racial identification: Give me the doll that… 5. looks like a white child 6. looks like a coloured child 7. looks like a Negro child	94% correct identification Misidentification more likely with younger children	Similar findings to Clarks	
Racial self-identification: Give me the doll that… 8. looks like you			
Behavioural consequences: What race is your best friend?	Not tested	No relationship found between doll preference and race of best friend for either race in both studies. Not tested in original Clarks' study.	

Gould 1982

Aim

To review the intelligence testing techniques used by Yerkes 1915 in order to highlight the problematic nature of intelligence testing.

Method

Yerkes used three tests:

- army Alpha: written test given to literate recruits;
- army Beta: men who were illiterate/failed the Alpha given a pictorial test;
- individual oral exam: failures on the Beta recalled for a spoken exam.

Cube Analysis. **How many cubes are there?**

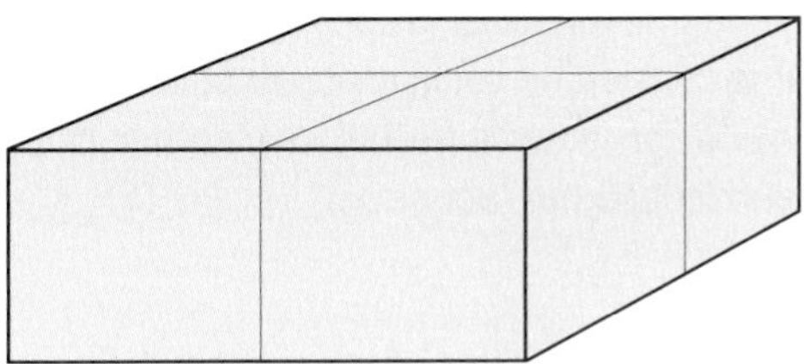

Example from the army Beta test

Participants: Yerkes originally tested 1.75 million army recruits during the First World War.

Results

Original findings

Three 'facts' were used by Boring and Brigham to support the idea of genetic differences between the races.

- Average mental age of white US just above moronity – 13.
- Possible to grade European immigrants by their country of origin.
- Average score of black men was 10.41 – below the white average.

Gould's findings

Gould argues that faulty conclusions had very negative implications:

- Intelligence can be objectively measured: assigned military positions and tasks accordingly.
- IQ tests can predict future performance: biased support for the argument that special educational measures were a waste of time and money.
- Intelligence is inherited: eugenics argument, e.g. selective breeding of highly intelligent humans – Immigration Restriction Act in 1924.

Methodological problems

Validity errors:

- Construct validity: lack of a clear operational definition of intelligence.
- Tests did not measure innate intelligence (native intellectual ability): questions were often based on American general knowledge.

Reliability errors:

- Unstandardised procedures were followed, e.g. many illiterate in English still given alpha test; failures on Alpha test often not recalled to take Beta test.

Interpretation of findings errors

- Ignored experience issue: the more experience a person had of the USA the higher their score – suggesting a cultural bias.
- Ignored education issue: positive correlation between number of years in education and test scores.

The ethics of socially sensitive research

- Illustrates the social consequences of psychological research: highlights the need to consider the political context of psychological theory.
- The debate continues: no good evidence to suggest IQ is genetic.

Quick test

1. ***Which experimental method was used by Hraba and Grant?***
2. ***What was the main difference in the dolls the black children wanted to play with between 1939 and 1969?***
3. ***Why did the black children in Clarks study prefer the white doll to play with?***
4. ***How did Gould question the validity of the IQ tests?***
5. ***What are the ethical issues related to IQ testing?***

1. A natural experiment (I/V was race of child). 2. In 1939, 67% of black children chose the white doll, compared with only 30% in 1969. 3. Clark suggests that this indicated that the children preferred to be white. 4. Construct validity – the construct of intelligence is not defined clearly. Not measuring 'native intelligence' – tests ignored educational and cultural issues. 5. Socially sensitive research – the impact of findings on the world, e.g. eugenics (selective breeding).

Defining psychological abnormality

Defining 'normality' and therefore 'abnormality' is both difficult and controversial. In the 17th century in Britain unusual behaviour was thought to be due to possession by the devil and individuals were often put to death! By the 18th century it was thought that they had 'lost their reason' and they were locked away in asylums. It wasn't until the 19th century that a more humane approach emerged with the first model – the 'medical model'. Other cultures have their own history and present approach to 'abnormality', which makes any model open to 'cultural relativism'.

Statistical infrequency

Abnormality is behaviour that is statistically rare in the general population.

Most people fall somewhere in the centre of this continuum but if an individual shows an extreme deviation then they may be regarded as abnormal.

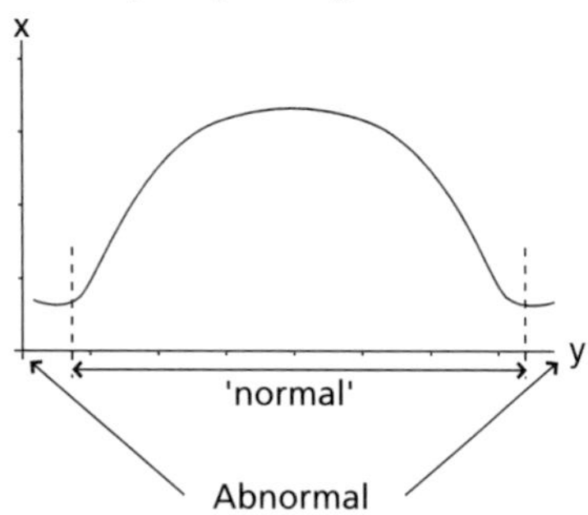

Strengths

- Objective measures that can be free from value judgements.

Limitations

- Still influenced by some value judgements, as there is a need to decide how far away from average constitutes 'abnormality' – 1, 2, 3 SDs?
- Deviations from average may in fact be desirable (e.g. genius, a low susceptibility to anxiety).
- Does not take into account cultural differences (or sub-cultural differences within a larger culture).

Deviation from social norms

Socially based definition. Social groups have their own ideas of what is considered socially acceptable behaviour. Any deviance away from these 'norms' is undesirable and labelled as 'abnormal'.

Strengths

- Takes into account the effect of 'abnormality' upon others.

Limitations

- Subjective definition of 'norm' for any given society. This can change over time, so an objective definition that is stable across cultures and time is difficult.
- Context in which behaviour occurs is important and depends upon many cultural and sub-cultural differences.

Failure to function adequately

Functioning adequately in day-to-day life without distress is considered 'normal' behaviour. Behaviours, mood or thinking that do not adequately cope with the world and that adversely affect the well-being of the individual are considered abnormal.

Strengths

- Takes into account the experience of the individual.
- Objective measures such as number of absences from work.

Limitations

- Individual may not be aware of their own dysfunction or distress.
- Social judgement is used. Other people may decide that functioning is inadequate and therefore will include personal and cultural bias.
- Difficulties in functioning adequately may be the result of social rejection.

Failure to function model

> **EXAMINER'S TOP TIP**
> Try to make a mnemonic from the initial letters of Rosenhan's model, e.g. Saw Many Very Unusual Insects On Vespas.

Rosenhan and Seligman 1989

This model has seven features:

- Suffering
- Maladaptive behaviour (prevents reaching goals)
- Unpredictability and loss of control
- Vividness and unconventionality of behaviour (relatively unusual)
- Irrationality and incomprehensibility
- Observer discomfort
- Violation of moral and ideal standards

Strengths

- Takes into account the experience of the individual and the effects on others.

Limitations

- Still involves subjective judgements.

Deviance from ideal mental health

- Jahoda (1958) described 'ideal mental health' as accurate perception of reality, self-acceptance, potential for growth and autonomy, and positive interpersonal relations and environmental mastery.
- Humanistic psychologists suggest that we all seek the same goals to meet needs, ranging from deficiency needs up to growth needs and finally reaching 'self-actualisation' (reaching one's full potential).
- Abnormality results from failure to achieve these goals.

Strengths

- Focus on positive characteristics rather than deficits or dysfunctions.
- Focus on the individual experience of mental health.

Limitations

- Abstract and culturally relative ideals, not shared by collectivistic societies.
- Measuring signs of psychological health are not easy and can only be subjective opinion of individuals.

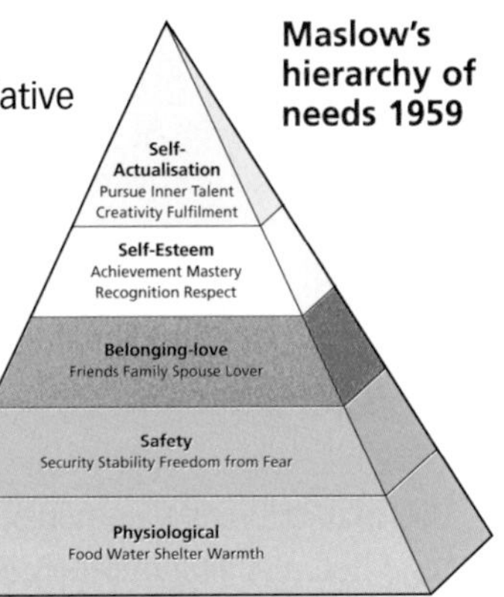

Cultural relativism

- Ongoing issue in any attempt to define psychological abnormality.
- Cultural universals do exist: e.g. chronic depression and anti-social behaviour are both considered abnormal in any culture.
- However, most definitions involve some subjective interpretation of behaviour, influenced by culturally determined values and judgements.
- Combined approach – objective measures along with a view of the experience from the aspect of the individual experiencing it.

Quick test

1. ***According to the statistical infrequency model, when might an individual be regarded as abnormal?***
2. ***Social 'norms' change in two ways: across cultures and what else?***
3. ***Why is the 'failure to function' model open to personal and cultural bias?***
4. ***What is an objective measure of the 'failure to function' model?***
5. ***What sort of culture would consider autonomy as abnormal?***
6. ***What is 'cultural relativism'?***

1. If an individual shows an extreme deviation from average. 2. They change over time. 3. Social judgement is used: others may decide when functioning is inadequate. 4. Absenteeism from work. 5. A collectivist society. 6. Definitions of abnormality involve some subjective interpretation of behaviour: this is influenced by cultural values and judgements.

Models of abnormality

Models provide assumptions about the causes of mental disorders and the treatment required for relief. They can be either biological (advocated by psychiatrists) or psychological (favoured by psychologists – psychodynamic, behaviourist or cognitive). All models provide a focus on a particular causal factor whilst ignoring others. The multi-dimensional stress-diathesis model attempts to integrate both approaches.

EXAMINER'S TOP TIP
A definition of abnormality is not the same as a model: know the difference.

Biological approach – the medical model

Main determinant of abnormality is dysfunctional brain activity or a chemical imbalance – same causes as a physical illness.

- Genetics: **Kendler, Masterson and Davis 1985** found that relatives of schizophrenics were 18 times more likely to develop schizophrenia than average.
- Infection: **Barr et al. 1990** found that the incidence of schizophrenia was increased in children whose mothers had flu when pregnant.

Treatment

- Symptoms can be identified, a diagnosis made and treatment given.
- Drugs, psychosurgery and electroconvulsive therapy can be very effective.
- Use of sectioning – compulsory detention and treatment of those regarded as being mentally ill.

Limitations

- Disorders with psychological symptoms – e.g. eating disorders – may be less easy to diagnose with this model (see pages 88–89).
- Physical treatments, e.g. drug therapy can have unwanted side effects.

Ethical implications

Positive

- Being mentally 'ill' means individual is not 'responsible' for their predicament.
- As a victim of circumstance they require treatment and care, not blame and stigmatism.

Negative

- Sectioning – power is with society and not individual – may lose rights and ability to consent to treatment.
- May lead to wrong diagnosis and treatment.
- May lead to 'labelling' and prejudice.

Diagnostic classification is necessary to identify groups or patterns of behaviour. *The Diagnostic and Statistical Manual of Mental Disorder (DSM-IV)* is a classification system used by the American Psychiatric Association.

Psychological approach – the psychodynamic model

- Imbalance between id, ego and superego. Present to a certain degree in everybody. Abnormality is a matter of quantity rather than quality.
- Abnormality can result from unresolved conflicts from childhood (e.g. Oedipus complex) or from repressed traumatic experiences (see **Freud**, page 44).

Treatment

Talking therapies encourage the individual to revisit their past and retrieve repressed memories. This works best for individuals who have insight into their own difficulties.

Limitations

Treatment is voluntary (and expensive) but can be very disturbing as it uncovers traumatic memories. It focuses on the past and ignores the present situation.

- Can focus too much on sexual problems rather than social difficulties.
- Little evidence of effectiveness: often based on single case studies.

Ethical implications

Positive

- Humane treatment: does not blame individuals and no institutionalisation.

Negative

- False memory syndrome (Loftus and Palmer, page 27)

Psychological approach – *the behaviourist model*

Maladaptive behaviour is learned through conditioning or observation. Abnormality is an observable, behavioural disorder.

Treatment

- **Directive therapy** consisting of re-programming individual with adaptive behaviours.
- Behaviour that is learned can also be unlearned.

Classical conditioning

- **Desensitisation**: slow but increasing presentation to the anxiety-provoking situation.
- **Aversion therapy**: previously enjoyed behaviours are associated with unpleasant consequences.

Operant conditioning

- Token economies: 'normal' or desirable behaviours are rewarded.
- 'Abnormal' behaviour is ignored as much as possible.

Limitations

- Reductionist: over-simplified and ignores complexities of human nature.
- Useful for treating external behaviours such as phobias but may not deal with underlying causes.
- Can be stressful, e.g. aversion therapy or flooding.
- Relies heavily on the behaviour of others, and learnt behaviours may not be transferred to new situations.

Ethical implications

Positive

- Lack of blame placed on the individual.
- Individual behaviours are targeted: the whole individual is not labelled.

Negative

- Treatment is dehumanising and manipulative and can be painful.

Psychological approach – *the cognitive model*

Irrational or distorted beliefs, which are difficult to control, about the self, others or the environment.

Treatment

- **Cognitive restructuring**: therapy helps patient develop rational and undistorted thoughts.
- **Stress inoculation training**: Meichenbaum 1977 – techniques for management and coping focusing on developing a more positive internal dialogue that can handle stressful situations.
- **Beck's cognitive treatment for depression**: three thought processes make up the **cognitive triad**

  Thoughts about self (*helpless, worthless and inadequate*)

  Thoughts about world (*negative and defeatist*)

  Thoughts about future (*hopeless*)
- Uncovering and challenging the negative and unrealistic beliefs of the depressed individual, e.g. by pointing out times when they have not felt helpless.

Limitations

- Uncertainty over whether distorted thinking is a cause or an effect of the disorder.

Ethical implications

Positive

- No institutionalisation is required.

Negative

- Individuals blamed for their own problems.
- Rational emotive therapy can be disturbing, although most cognitive therapy is humane.

The multi-dimensional approach

The diathesis-stress model states that bothgenetic factors and environmental stress are necessary for mental disorders to develop.

Diathesis = a genetic vulnerability to develop diseases or disorders

Sress = a severe or disturbing evironmental stress.

Quick test

1. *What are the two main categories of models of abnormality?*
2. *What are the main treatments for abnormality in the biological approach?*
3. *Why is abnormality a matter of quantity rather than quality in the psychodynamic approach?*
4. *What are the positive ethical implications of the behavioural approach?*
5. *Why is the diathesis-stress model a multi-dimensional approach?*

1. Biological and psychological models. 2. Drugs, psychosurgery and electroconvulsive therapy. 3. An imbalance between id, ego and superego is present to a certain degree in everybody. 4. Lack of blame placed on the individual. 5. It combines biological and psychological aspects of abnormality.

Schizophrenia/MPD (Multiple Personality Disorder)

This spread covers two investigations:

- **'On being sane in insane places' (Rosenhan 1973).**
- **Multiple Personality Disorder (MPD) (Thigpen and Cleckley 1954).**

Rosenhan 1973

Aim

To illustrate experimentally the problems involved in determining normality and abnormality, in particular, the poor reliability of the diagnostic classification system (and its validity), the consequences of being diagnosed as abnormal and the effects of institutionalisation.

Method

Participant observation.

Attempted to gain admission to 12 different hospitals in five different states in the USA.

Participants: hospital staff.

Confederates: eight sane people – a graduate student, three psychologists, a paediatrician, a psychiatrist, a painter, a housewife (three women and five men).

Procedure

- Confederates arrived at admissions complaining of hearing voices.
- Simulated 'existential crisis' – 'Who am I, what's it all for?'
- After admission stopped simulating symptoms.
- Took part in ward activities – spent time writing notes.
- Had to get out by convincing staff they were sane.

Results

- All but one admitted with a diagnosis of schizophrenia – a mental disorder with the following symptoms: delusion, hallucinations, incoherent word associations, inappropriate emotions, lack of emotion.
- Remained in hospital for 7–52 days: eventually released with the label 'schizophrenia in remission'. (Stickiness of labels.)
- Not detected by any staff although many patients suspected their sanity.

General observations

- Lack of monitoring – nurses in office 90% of time and a strong sense of segregation.
- Distortion of behaviour – emotional instability, 'patient engages in writing behaviour', nervousness and oral acquisitive syndrome.
- Lack of normal interaction: 71% of psychiatrists and 88% of nurses walked on, averting their gaze when asked a simple question.
- Depersonalisation and powerlessness, e.g. lack of privacy.
- Medication: a total of 2 100 tablets given to all confederates.

Study 2

- Doctors may be strongly biased towards type-two errors (Scheffé 1966), i.e. more inclined to call a healthy person sick (a false positive) than a sick person healthy (a false negative: type-one error).
- Teaching hospital aware of first study informed that one or more pseudopatients would attempt to admit themselves.
- 41 out of 193 patients were spotted as pseudopatients – in fact they were all real patients!

Conclusions

- Confirms Rosenhan's initial hypothesis; it is the setting (situation) as much as the individual's behaviour (disposition) that leads to diagnosis.
- We cannot distinguish the sane from the insane in psychiatric hospitals!

Strengths

- Good ecological validity (but not the same as being a real patient).
- Low demand characteristics.

Weaknesses

- Lack of control group.
- Difficult to replicate.
- Difficult to generalise (USA only).
- Difficulties of recording accurate and prompt details whilst participating.

Ethics

- Deception of hospital staff.
- No right to withdraw.
- No informed consent.
- Psychological harm, as attention drawn to inability staff to diagnose abnormality.

Alternative

Self-reports from real patients would improve the ecological validity of the study and remove the biased opinion of pseudopatients.

EXAMINER'S TOP TIP

Evaluation of studies will gain higher marks than simple description.

Thigpen and Cleckley 1954

Aim

To discover if MPD exists.

Method

Case study (using self-reports – interviews).

Participant: Eve White.

Case study

- Eve White had 'blackouts', memory loss, marital conflicts and perennial frustrations.
- Therapists used hypnosis to restore memory.
- A letter was received containing two different types of handwriting – White denied sending this.
- One visit she suddenly appeared to be someone else (Eve Black), with a completely different personality.
- Black could be 'called out' when White was under hypnosis.
- White was only aware of Black when told by therapists. She was then able to negotiate with Black for time.
- After White deteriorated, a third personality, Jane, emerged. Eve White's and Jane's EEG were in fact indistinguishable, although Eve Black's was different.
- In 1975 the real Eve came forward: Christine Sizemore – she reported there had been 22 personalities altogether.

Results

Differences found between White and Black:

Eve White	Eve Black
Demure and retiring	Confident and relaxed
IQ = 110	IQ = 104
Superior memory	Inferior memory
Repressive personality (Rorschach test)	Regressive personality

Strengths

- Case study: researchers got to know Eve White well and collected in-depth data.
- They assert that a performance could not have continued so long and so consistently.

Weaknesses

- Problems of conducting action research: expectation effects, therapist effects.
- Thigpen described White as boring and colourless and Black as irrepressible, naughty and sensual. He was quite taken with Eve Black – could he have given her unconscious signals?
- Culturally specific: MPD could be regarded as a largely North American phenomenon of the 20th century.

Validity and reliability

- Questionable construct validity: is there any such thing as MPD?
- Reliability of tests questionable:
  - affected by deliberate attempts to fake;
  - EEGs objective, but open to interpretation;
  - IQ tests – questionable validity and reliability (see Gould, page 81);
  - projective tests – doubtful reliability due to subjective nature of interpretation.

Ethics

- Was informed consent gained from each personality?
- The ethical/moral dilemma of 'killing' one or more personalities.
- Causing psychological harm?

Applications

- Better understanding of mental health.
- Questions of moral/criminal responsibility.

An example from Rorschach test

Quick test

1. *Who were the participants in Rosenhan's study?*
2. *What did Rosenhan mean by 'the stickiness of labels'?*
3. *What are the strengths of conducting case studies?*
4. *What objective measures were used to compare White and Black?*
5. *Why is construct validity an issue in Thigpen and Cleckley's study?*

1. The hospital staff (note: not the 8 'sane' people). 2. The label of 'schizophrenia' sticks to the patient, i.e. only in remission – not cured. 3. Detailed and in-depth data. 4. IQ tests, Rorschach test, memory tests and EEGs. 5. Questions surrounding the existence of MPD – therefore unsure of what is being measured.

Eating disorders

Despite appearing in the *DSM III* in 1980, there is still debate on the existence of eating disorders. Increasing diagnosis means that now 0.5 to 3% of females in adolescence to early adulthood are diagnosed each year. Disorders occur more often in Western societies and in middle-class families and are 10 times more common in women than in men.

Clinical characteristics

Anorexia nervosa ('loss of appetite')

DSM IV states that four symptoms must be shown:

- **Behavioural**: weight – a refusal to maintain a body weight normal for age and height (85% of what is expected).
- **Emotional**: anxiety – an intense fear of gaining weight even though obviously under-weight.
- **Cognitive**: body-image distortion – over-estimation of body size and over-emphasis of its importance for self-esteem.
- **Somatic**: loss of body weight and absence of menstruation for three consecutive months (amenorrhoea).

Bulimia nervosa ('ox appetite')

Behavioural symptoms

- Recurring binge eating – excessive quantities consumed within a discrete period of time (about 2 hours) with a sense of being out of control.
- Recurring inappropriate compensatory behaviour – self-induced vomiting, misuse of laxatives, fasting or excessive exercise.
- Occurs on average at least twice a week for three months.

Cognitive symptoms

- Self-image overly influenced by body size and shape.

Unlike anorexia, bulimia sufferers usually maintain their weight within the normal range, although bulimia causes other damage to their bodies. Bulimics are trying to satisfy a constant craving; anorexics are striving toward perfection.

Biological explanations

Genetics

Anorexia and bulimia may be passed on through genes.

Research studies – twin studies

Holland et al. 1984 found the chance of both twins developing eating disorders was:

- MZ identical twins – 55%;
- DZ non-identical twins – 7%.

Kendler et al. 1991 reported concordance rates of 23% for MZ twins and 8.7% for DZ twins with bulimia.

Evaluation

- Concordance rates are not 100% for MZ twins, suggesting environmental factors are also involved. Genes may predispose individual to developing disorders.
- Alternative studies: adoption of twins – control for environmental influences.
- Does not explain the recent major increase in sufferers.

Physiology

Research studies

- Hypothalamus: **Garfinkel and Garner 1982** suggest disturbed hypothalamic functioning. Removal of the lateral hypothalamus in rats caused them to refuse to eat, whilst ablating the hypothalamus caused them to overeat until they became obese.
- Biochemical: **Fava et al. 1989** found links between levels of neurotransmitters/hormones and eating disorders (serotonin and noradrenaline).

Evaluation

- Post-mortem studies have not revealed damage in the hypothalamus.
- It is difficult to identify cause and effect, e.g. is the biochemical imbalance causing the disorder or is it an effect of starvation and purging?
- Anti-depressants that increase serotonin levels are effective in treating bulimia.

Cognitive theory

Cognitive biases

- Distorted perception of body shape and weight, irrational attitudes towards eating habits and dieting (e.g. the disinhibition hypothesis).
- May be seeking to assert control over their lives idealistically and to reach perfection.

Research studies

- Garfinkel and Garner 1982: used an image-distorting technique to establish the perceptions of anorexics – most over-estimated their body size.
- Dura and Bornstein 1989: academic achievements much higher than IQ scores would predict, suggesting the drive for perfection extends to other areas.

Evaluation

- Difficult to identify cause and effect: are cognitive biases causes of eating disorders or effects of them?

Behaviourist theory

All behaviour is learned in some way: society and culture determine individuals' behaviour.

Research studies

- **Classical conditioning**: eating associated with anxiety – a weight gain phobia develops (Leitenberg et al. 1968).
- **Operant conditioning**: reinforcement for eating behaviour – social praise or respect from a society that places a high value on slimness; attention and concern may be reinforcing.
- **Social learning theory**: thin role models will be imitated. Over half of Miss America contestants were 15% below expected weight – Barlow and Durand 1995.

Evaluation

- Behaviour modification therapy supports these explanations.
- Explains cultural specificity and the rise in incidence in recent years.
- Does not explain why not all women develop eating disorders.

Psychological models

Psychodynamic approach

One explanation is that eating disorders are a means of avoiding adult maturity, as the adolescent attempts to remain in a 'child-like' appearance. Another explanation focuses around the interactions between family members. Eating disorders are seen as a symptom of hidden conflict within the family – family therapy can be helpful.

Research studies

- Minuchin's family systems theory (1978): anorexia develops as a result of enmeshed family dynamics. The child is not allowed to become independent, as their role is vital in the identities of other family members (e.g. caring parent).
- Bruch (1971): anorexia is related to mother-daughter conflicts over autonomy, and food can become a battleground for dominance and control.

Evaluation

- Cause and effect cannot be identified.
- Case studies only – no objective research.
- Cannot explain recent increases in the incidence of these disorders.

EXAMINER'S TOP TIP

Debate the research support for each approach. Consider the strengths and weaknesses of each.

Quick test

1. ***What are the cognitive symptoms associated with anorexia?***
2. ***What are the main differences between anorexia and bulimia?***
3. ***Why are MZ twins often used in studying the genetic basis for eating disorders?***
4. ***What is the main difficulty with studying eating disorders?***
5. ***According to the psychodynamic approach, what is at stake if the anorexic sufferer becomes well again?***
6. ***Who is more likely to suffer from eating disorders?***

1. Body-image distortion: over-estimation of body size and over-emphasis of its importance for self-esteem. 2. Anorexics are 85% underweight, bulimics normal weight; anorexics are striving toward perfection, bulimics to satisfy a constant craving. 3. Identical genes – concurrence of traits suggests genetic factors are involved. 4. Identifying causal relationships. 5. The 'identities' of all family members – e.g. mother can no longer be the concerned caregiver. 6. Women, middle class and westerners.

Practice questions

Use these to test your progress. Check your answers on pages 92–95.

Individual differences

1 What is meant by the term 'sex-role stereotype'? [2]

2 Describe the main features of cultural diversity in gender roles. [3]

3 Describe the main difference between biological explanations and social learning explanations for gender role behaviour. [2]

4 Outline two features of gender bias in theory and research. [2]

5 Evaluate the study by Hraba and Grant. [2]

6 Outline the findings of Gould's study into 'intelligence'. [3]

7 Describe the 'statistical infrequency' explanation of abnormality. [2]

8 Describe the 'failure to function' explanation of abnormality. [2]

9 What are the seven features of Rosenhan and Seligman's 1989 failure to function model? [4]

10 What are the limitations of the humanistic approach to abnormality? [2]

11 Outline the medical model of abnormality. [3]

12 Describe the behaviourist approach to abnormality. [2]

13 Describe Beck's cognitive treatment for depression. [2]

....

....

14 What is the 'diathesis-stress' model of abnormality? [2]

....

15 What conclusion did Rosenhan reach in his study of abnormality? [2]

....

....

16 Evaluate the ethics of Rosenhan's study. [3]

....

17 Evaluate the reliability of the tests used to assess MPD by Thigpen and Cleckley. [2]

....

....

18 What are the problems of conducting action research? [2]

....

....

19 What is meant by the term 'anorexia nervosa'? [2]

....

20 How many symptoms must be shown for a diagnosis of anorexia to be made and what are they? [3]

....

....

21 What is meant by the term 'bulimia nervosa'? [2]

....

22 What are the behavioural symptoms of bulimia nervosa? [2]

....

23 Evaluate the evidence that anorexia and bulimia may be passed on in families through genes. [4]

....

....

24 To what extent are distorted cognitions the cause of eating disorders? [4]

....

....

25 To what extent are eating disorders learned behaviour? [4]

....

....

Total /63

Answers

Research methods in psychology (pages 20–21)

1 To test theories and look for differences between conditions.
2 Variables are anything that varies. The independent variable is the variable that is manipulated before the experiment to see what affect this has on the dependent variable.
3 Other variables that could also influence the dependent variable. They must be kept constant to ensure they do not confound the results.
4 To ensure extraneous variables do not influence results and to increase reliability.
5 The extent to which the results of an experiment can be generalised to other situations in real life.
6 In a field experiment the I/V is deliberately manipulated in a real-life setting. In a natural experiment the I/V is naturally occurring.
7 Observing naturally occurring behaviour in the participants' natural environment. There is no manipulation of variables.
8 Detailed and in-depth data recorded. Ecological validity depends upon how integrated with the participant the researcher has become. The researcher's presence influences the participant's behaviour. Problems with recording data promptly and ethical issues of deception.
9 If two or more observers are used the chances of biased results are reduced and inter-observer reliability can be checked.
10 Biased by social desirability and motivational levels. Bias due to acquiescence or to response set. Cause and effect cannot be identified. Answers need interpretation. Can rely on a person's memory of events, thoughts and feelings and therefore are prone to unreliable answers.
11 A hypothesis that predicts the direction of the effect.
12 A statement predicting that the results of the study will be due to chance alone and not due to the effects of the independent variable.
13 Through the use of inferential tests.
14 Validity in general is the extent to which the experiment measures what it is supposed to measure. Construct validity is validating a hypothetical construct, e.g. intelligence.
15 Split-half method or test-retest method.
16 Order effects (if one participant does both conditions they may become practised at the task or bored with it). Eliminated by counter-balancing or randomisation.
17 A random sample, where each person in a given population stands an equal chance of being selected for inclusion.
18 Different participants are used in each condition of the experiment. Order effects are not an issue and demand characteristics are less of an issue than repeated measures. Large sample is needed and individual differences between participants could confound the results.
19 Attempts to eliminate participant expectations by giving a control group a treatment that should have no effect.
20 Gain informed consent, no deception, debriefing afterwards, the right to withdraw, protection of participants from harm, confidentiality and be aware of socially sensitive research.
21 Stay within the law (e.g. cannot cause pain or distress), weigh up the costs and rewards, seek permission from the Home Office. Consider the needs of the species (e.g. no endangered species; is another species likely to suffer less), caging conditions.
22 Data in descriptive form. Researcher bias, subjective interpretation and difficult to analyse.
23 If scores can be ordered (ordinal, interval or ratio).
24 Does not show cause and effect.
25 A statistical calculation used to give a more precise measure of the relationship between two variables and the degree of probability.

Cognitive psychology (pages 34–35)

1 How information is stored, e.g. acoustically (sound) in STM or semantically (meaning) in LTM.
2 Because of acoustic confusion errors – Conrad 1964.
3 Seven (plus or minus two) – Miller 1956.
4 Knowing *that* something is true (e.g. facts).
5 Too simplistic and inflexible and not true to real-life memory performance.
6 The Central Executive.
7 Depth of processing through MODE – meaning, organisation, distinctiveness and elaboration.
8 Forgetting: in STM seems to be due to decay or displacement, whereas LTM it seems to be due to retrieval failure or interference.
9 A limited capacity store can lose information because it has been replaced by newer material.
10 New information interferes with old information.
11 All studies use laboratory experiments and therefore lack ecological validity.
12 Cues in the environment (external) act as cues for jogging the memory (Abernethy 1940), as can internal cues such as mood state.
13 Highly emotional states can improve memory, perhaps because of hormones produced at the time (e.g. the death of Princess Diana).
14 Testimony unreliable due to reconstructive nature of memory:
Schema theory – Bartlett – evidence from 'War of the Ghosts' showed changes after 20 hours. However, lacks of experimental control and it cannot account for occasions when memory is extremely accurate.
Unreliable testimony due to the influence of language on memory (leading questions – Loftus and Palmer): Evidence from laboratory studies shows how the verb 'smashed' increases estimates of speed and the likelihood of seeing broken glass that was not present. However, biased samples, reliance on self-reports and lack of ecological validity.
15 Most evidence suggests perception is learned – cross-cultural studies find individual differences and not cultural universals.
16 Attention is on single channel in both but Triesman suggests that unselected channels are weakened, not blocked out completely (Broadbent).
17 Africans did not use any depth cues (two-dimensional viewers).
18 Devising a method in one culture and using it on another culture (e.g. Africans unfamiliar with pictures drawn on paper).
19 Semanticity, displacement, structure dependence, creativity, generalisation.

20 Noam Chomsky – we are born with an innate Language Acquisition Device (LAD) – therefore due to nature.
21 Chimps had no increase in length of sentences but increase in imitation – other way round for children. Also, children's utterances are more spontaneous and they can learn to take turns, which chimps do not.
22 Removed from home and family at a young age and bought up in 'unnatural' environment.
23 Instrumental learning – reinforcement.
24 At age 4 years she had learned 132 signs. She used displacement, semanticity, creativity, generalisation but not structure dependence.
25 The ability to understand that other people may have a different belief to yours.

Developmental psychology (pages 48–49)

1 Pre-attachment (asocial), indiscriminate attachment and specific attachments.
2 A long-lasting, close and strong bond between two people.
3 Secure/insecure (anxious-resistant, anxious-avoidant and disorganised).
4 Parental sensitivity, infant temperament, family circumstances and cross-cultural differences in child rearing.
5 It is based upon American cultural assumptions about behaviour.
6 Attachment ensures a greater likelihood of their offspring surviving and thus their own genes being passed on.
7 Data relies heavily on retrospective self-reports: unreliable memories plus socially desirability effects.
8 Attachments, and relationships generally, are learned through imitation plus some mental processing.
9 Syndrome of distress (Protest, Despair, Detachment model) – Robertson's films of children in hospital.
10 A break in the bond during the early years will have serious and irreversible effects on the cognitive, emotional and social development of the child.
11 Loss of appetite, apathy and a sense of resigned helplessness seen in deprived children.
12 It uses retrospective data, studies only short periods of separation and only finds correlations. The issue of researcher expectations may have influenced results.
13 Bowlby suggests maternal deprivation, whilst Rutter proposed other factors such as family discord or poor living conditions.
14 Characteristics of the child (temperament, age, gender) and previous experience (type of attachment to parent, experience of separation, attachment to others and the quality of care).
15 Correlation found between delinquency and psychiatric illness in caregiver or discord within the family: no delinquency found when separation was due to other reasons, e.g. physical illness or death of the mother.
16 Privation in the early years of life leads to underdevelopment of cognitive skills, language and social skills.
17 Hodges and Tizard's study of adoption. Freud and Dann's children in concentration camp improved intellectually (although still emotionally underdeveloped). Harlow's Rhesus monkeys developed normally if allowed to play with other monkeys of their own age.
18 Yes; they can make attachments later on but depends on adults concerned and how much they nurture such attachments.
19 Learning can take place by observation without any classical or operant conditioning. Children more likely to learn from same-sex models through the process of identification.
20 Both: the biological id comes into conflict with demands of the environment.
21 Little Hans asking mother to powder his penis, anxiety over losing his mother, fear of bath, dream of taking small giraffe away from large giraffe, fear of heavily loaded carts.
22 Informed consent from parent not child. Protection of children may be more difficult. Emotional distress? Debriefing – child may not understand.
23 More stimulation, interaction and educational activities Burchinal et al. – positive correlation between pre-school day care and IQ levels upon entering school.
24 Privation or deprivation effects. Belsky and Rovine 1988 found infants were more likely to develop insecure attachments if they received day care for over 20 hours per week before they were a year old. Kagan et al 1980 – found no significantly consistent differences.
25 Correlations don't show causal relationships; validity of tests (e.g. SS or IQ). Findings useful for applications to ensure consistency in day care; e.g. low staff turnover, use of 'key workers' and in-service training.

Social psychology (pages 62–63)

1 Obedience is to do as instructed, usually in response to an individual (a leader), whilst conformity is to follow group norms.
2 Well-controlled lab studies (identify causal relationships) but can lack ecological validity. Studies are often culturally and historically biased.
3 Culture (historical, ethnicity) – Smith and Bond 1993. Deindividuation: loss of a sense of personal identity (Zimbardo 1969).
4 If behaviour of minority is consistently different from majority (internal causes), their opinions are considered serious and sincere. Flexibility (Nemeth et al.), commitment and relevance are also important.
5 Set in a more realistic setting (hospital) where the nurses did not know they were being studied.
6 Bickman (1974) – guard, milkman or man in sports coat asked passers-by to 'pick up bag'; more people complied with the request from the guard than from the others.
7 Dispositional explanations: within the individual, e.g. Adorno et al. 1950. Authoritarian personality: rigid beliefs in conventional values, submissive attitudes towards authority figures, general hostility towards other groups and intolerance of ambiguity – more likely to be prejudiced and more likely to obey an authority figure.
8 Location of the study, purpose of the experiment, social obligations, payment, the unusual nature of the task they were performing, the tendency for people to accept the commands of people in authority.
9 Use of deception, right to withdraw and psychological distress caused to participants. However, tests confirmed participants were unharmed and they were fully debriefed. Endorsed by the American Psychological Association and has contributed to our understanding – do 'the ends justify the means'?

10 The similarity of the laboratory experiment to events that commonly happen to people in the real world – Orne and Holland.
11 Milgram suggests that the participants were clearly experiencing real distress at the situation and therefore were taking the situation seriously.
12 Bickman's findings were not replicated in other situations, whereas Milgram's were – and this is the criterion for a study to be ecologically valid.
13 Our perceptions of others are influenced strongly by our perceptions of ourself.
14 Traits that appear first can have more impact in final impression (first impressions).
15 A rigid prototype applied to large social groups, which ranks the group in a social hierarchy or stratification system.
16 Stereotyped explanations based on our past experience. Multiple sufficient causes, where any number of causes are sufficient to cause behaviour and multiple necessary causes, where many causes are needed to produce behaviour – Kelley's causal schemata model (1972).
17 Most participants felt experiment was real: they adopted behaviour appropriate to their role.
18 Source must be credible, attractive and similar to oneself. The argument must appeal to emotions and the audience should be of similar intelligence, gender, age and culture.
19 A means to an end: genuine competition between groups with divergent interests, e.g. scarce social resources – housing, jobs. E.g. Sherif's Robber's cave study (1961)
20 The tendency to feel hostility towards out-group members and to undervalue the products of an out-group. Also the tendency for increased liking of in-group members plus pressure for conformity and group cohesion, and to overvalue the products of an in-group.
21 Merely being categorised is enough to create intergroup rivalry. Discriminatory behaviour can be expected even if no prejudiced attitudes are present.
22 Discriminatory behaviour was measured by counting the rewards each boy gave to in-group members and out-group members using the matrices.
23 Individual weighs up the costs of helping against the costs of not helping and the rewards of helping against the rewards of not helping.
24 By gaining 'prior general consent' (a pool of volunteers consent to being deceived in some future experiment) or 'presumptive consent' (approval from the general public can be gained prior to an experiment), e.g. Gamson et al. 1982.
25 The results of social research may be used by others: for this reason the publication of results should be carefully thought through beforehand and the consequences considered.

Physiological psychology (pages 76–77)

1 Thinking and planning, controlling fine voluntary movement.
2 Emotion and motivation, relaying information from senses to the cortex (thalamus).
3 MRI scans, PET scans, EEGs, accidental or deliberate damage, electrical stimulation.
4 Objective – free from personal bias; controlled – the use of controlled conditions; replicable – being able to repeat the study in exactly same way; and refutable – using aims and hypotheses that can be tested.
5 Positive: objective measures and recorded subjective dreams (avoiding experimenter bias and demand characteristics). Negative: biased sample, unreliable self-reports, lack of ecological validity and lack of control over I/V.
6 Physiological arousal (epinephrine injection or placebo); explanation of arousal (informed, misinformed, or ignorant); social cues (euphoric or angry stooge).
7 'Cognitive labelling theory' – people label their emotional state according to available cognitions (influenced by social situation). If there is no physiological arousal, cognitive cues to emotion have no effect.
8 Demand characteristics were particularly problematic for the angry condition – participants risked not gaining extra points on an exam if they owned up to feeling angry.
9 That each hemisphere has slightly different functions, possesses an independent stream of conscious awareness and has its own set of memories that are inaccessible to the other.
10 Questions over construct validity (lateralised brain function). Lack of control over variables such as individual differences and a biased (atypical) sample.
11 The independent variable (murderer/non-murderer) is naturally occurring.
12 The limbic system – in particular the amygdala.
13 NGRI have significant differences in glucose metabolism in selected brain regions: in particular in the pre-frontal cortex, parietal cortex, corpus callosum, amygdala, hippocampus and thalamus.
14 A state that occurs when people are faced with demands from their environment that they think they can't meet.
15 It pumps adrenaline into the bloodstream to provide energy and leads to the 'fight or flight' response.
16 In general a heightened sense of arousal will have a detrimental effect on our health, such as reducing the effectiveness of the immune system and increasing the risk of cardiovascular disease (heart attacks) and stomach ulcers, which can lead to death.
17 Proposes the same response regardless of type of stressor and its severity and duration. Ignores individual differences in coping mechanisms.
18 Triggers the adrenal gland to produce adrenaline and steroid hormones. The adrenaline triggers the activation of the sympathetic nervous system (fight/flight response) and the steroid hormone produces a steady supply of glucose.
19 Ambient (ever-present), cataclysmic (extreme and sudden disaster), and personal stressors (such as the death of a loved one or everyday hassles).
20 Fear of losing one's job, punitive management, interpersonal conflict and lack of control over one's role – role conflict and role ambiguity. Work overload can lead to 'burnout'.
21 Holmes and Rahe used the Social Readjustment Rating Scale, which asked people to indicate events they had been part of in the previous 12 months. Each event had been previously rated according to how long it was commonly considered necessary for a person to readjust. A score of over 300 indicates the person is at risk of mental and physical illness.
22 Gender: men worse – more heart attacks, less social support, less healthier lifestyle. Culture: e.g. Weg 1983 (Russia) – genetic factors and healthy lifestyle; urban areas – higher blood pressure (Cooper 1999).

Personality: e.g. Friedman and Rosenman 1959 – Type A (competitive and ambitious) more likely to suffer from stress.

23 Difference between perceived demands and perceived coping strategies, e.g. Langer and Rodin 1976, study in nursing home. Internal locus of control – cope better as can take control of situation (Rotter 1962). Behaviour constraint theory (Proshansky 1970) – perceived loss of control leads to learned helplessness (Seligman). Evidence is theoretical, empirical support from Langer and Rodin only. Seligman's study lacks generalisability to humans. However, application of theory does produce better coping strategies.

Individual differences (pages 90–91)

1 An 'overgeneralisation' of what behaviour is culturally acceptable for one gender or another: e.g. masculine = instrumental traits and feminine = expressive traits.

2 Most societies promote instrumental traits in males and expressive traits in females – but great diversity exists. Cultural relativism (e.g. Mead 1935) – gender roles depend upon the society, e.g. members of a New Guinea tribe (Tchambuli) showed the reverse of Western stereotypical gender roles.

3 Biological theory emphasises nature (role of chromosomes and testosterone/oestrogen) whilst social learning theory emphasises nurture, the role of learning from social models with which we identify.

4 Androcentric (male-biased views) are used as the 'norm': behaviour that does not fit this norm is often not investigated. Researchers, sample of participants and the interpretation and publication of the results are all male-dominated areas.

5 Good concurrent validity and replicable. Different towns and forced choice, so may lack validity. Lack of generalisability.

6 Negative implications of faulty conclusions such as eugenics: Yerkes' original IQ tests lacked construct validity and were culturally biased. Lack of reliability: procedure was unstandardised. Ignored educational and experience issues.

7 Abnormality is behaviour that is statistically rare in the general population.

8 Behaviours, mood or thinking that do not adequately cope with the world and that adversely affect the well-being of the individual are considered abnormal.

9 Remember your mnemonic: suffering; maladaptive behaviour (prevents reaching goals); vividness and unconventionality of behaviour (relatively unusual); unpredictability and loss of control; irrationality and incomprehensibility; observer discomfort; violation of moral and ideal standards.

10 Abstract and culturally relative ideals, not shared by collectivistic societies. Measuring signs of psychological health are not easy and can only be the subjective opinion of individuals.

11 The medical model: dysfunctional brain activity or a chemical imbalance have the same causes as a physical illness. Genetics (e.g. Kendler et al. 1985); infection (e.g. Barr et al. 1990). Biological treatment focuses on changing physical brain activity.

12 Abnormality is learned through conditioning or observation. Treatment focuses on directive therapy, consisting of re-programming individual with adaptive behaviours.

13 Three thought processes make up the cognitive triad: the self, the world and the future. Treatment: uncovering and challenging the negative and unrealistic beliefs of depressed individual, e.g. pointing out times when they have not felt helpless.

14 A multi-dimensional approach: both genetic factors and environmental stress are necessary for mental disorders to develop.

15 We cannot distinguish the sane from the insane in psychiatric hospitals! It is the situation as much as the individual's behaviour (disposition) that leads to a diagnosis of abnormality.

16 Deception of hospital staff, no right to withdraw, no informed consent, psychological harm as attention drawn to inability to staff to diagnose abnormality.

17 Affected by deliberate attempts to fake; EEGs are objective tests, but still open to interpretation; IQ tests have questionable validity and reliability (see Gould); projective tests have doubtful reliability due to the subjective nature of their interpretation.

18 Expectation effects, therapist effects. Could Thigpen be giving Eve Black unconscious signals? Attempting to change something whilst investigating it.

19 Loss of appetite.

20 Four: behavioural (85% of expected weight); emotional – anxiety over gaining weight; cognitive – body-image distortion; somatic – loss of weight and absence of menstruation.

21 Ox appetite.

22 Recurring binge eating and inappropriate compensatory behaviour occurring on average at least twice a week for three months.

23 Holland et al. 1984 found concordance rates in MZ twins to be 55%; Kendler 1991 found 23% concordance. However, this is not 100%, suggesting that environmental factors are also involved. Genes may predispose individual to developing disorders (diathesis-stress model). Does not explain the major increase in sufferers in recent years.

24 Cognitive biases such as distorted perception of body shape and attempts to reach perfection. Studied by Garfinkel and Garner 1982, who used an image-distorting technique to gain the perceptions of anorexics – most over-estimated their body size. Bura and Bornstein 1989 – academic achievements much higher than IQ scores would predict, suggesting the drive for perfection extends to other areas. Difficult to identify cause and effect: are cognitive biases a cause of eating disorders or an effect of them?

25 Classical conditioning such as phobias (Leitenberg 1968); operant conditioning such as reinforcement consequences for eating behaviour; social learning theory – thin role models will be imitated. Over half of Miss America contestants were 15% below expected weight (Barlow and Durand 1995). Behaviour modification therapy supports these explanations. Explains the cultural specificity and the rise in incidence in recent years. However, does not explain why not all women develop eating disorders.

Index